I ALL
NEED
TO KNOW,
I LEARNED
IN YESHIVA

ALL I NEED TO KNOW, I LEARNED IN YESHIVA

Yaakov Wolfson

TARGUM/FELDHEIM

First published 1995
Copyright © 1995 by Yaakov Wolfson
ISBN 1-56871-083-6

Phototypeset at Targum Press
Printing plates by Frank, Jerusalem

Published by:
Targum Press Inc.
22700 W. Eleven Mile Rd.
Southfield, Mich. 48034

Distributed by:
Feldheim Publishers
200 Airport Executive Park
Nanuet, N.Y. 10954

Distributed in Israel by:
Targum Press Ltd.
POB 43170
Jerusalem 91430

Printed in Israel

לע"נ

ר' יחיאל מיכל ב"ר אברהם דוד ז"ל
וזוגי שרה ע"ה

מוקירי תורה. רחימי רבנן.
חבל על דאבדין ולא משתכחין.

ת. נ. צ. ב. ה.

Table of Contents

Acknowledgments

*I*T IS WITH HEARTFELT APPRECIATION that I give credit and thanks to those who have helped in the publication of this book directly and indirectly, in different ways and at different times.

My *roshei yeshivos* and *rabbeim* have directed me, nurtured me, and encouraged me to the aspirations this book projects.

I will try to live their ideals.

My parents were the force of encouragement and perseverance behind this project and have given to me continuously of themselves. I can merely say that I am *makir* the *tov* of their giving.

My deepest gratitude to a true friend who has preferred anonymity: you were undoubtedly the *staying* force behind this book's publication.

My heartfelt thanks to Rabbi Yaakov Yosef Reinman, who directed this book through its initial stages, truly creating a book from a collection of essays.

Kudos to the Targum Press staff for putting their expertise to bear — quickly, efficiently, and decisively.

And thank you, thank you so very much...Hashem.

Yaakov Wolfson
Brooklyn, N.Y.
Nissan 5755

Foreword

*I*DEALISM HAS ALWAYS FOUND its strength in youth. From the scores of environmentalist movements to the many human-rights "watchdog" groups, youth have always played a dominant role. Young people, it would seem, have a vision of a better world — a world of people living in harmony, a world of caring and sharing — and are determined to do whatever it will take to bring that world into reality.

But as they get older, they begin to understand that the world is not a perfect place; it never has been. Eventually, they concede that they will not be able to change that.

I am young, and I am idealistic.

Yet the idealism I advocate is different from the general understanding of the word. I am not trying to change the world. I am not trying to ban the production of cigarettes, to get New Yorkers to clean up New York, or to "bring peace and brotherhood between Jew and

Arab in the Holy Land." I am simply trying to live my own life in the way I am best off living it, in a lifestyle that will be the ideal.

It is difficult to have the concept of direction in life on your mind when there are individual needs that must be addressed: bills to be paid, faucets to be fixed, shopping to be done.

It is also very hard to be idealistic when there is nothing holding you to it. Over the years, daily life begins to settle into familiar patterns, and the aspirations of youth have a way of diminishing.

It is for these reasons that I have written these essays. They contain the means to help us clear our sights and reset our goals, and they express standards we can strive to maintain.

In "Part One: Reflections," I have tried to bring out points on a mix of topics. Some of the stories are true, some of them are not, and some contain fictionalized details (such as the Ahavas Achim synagogue described in "Out-of-Town Kollel"), but in any case the story is only a vehicle through which to deliver a point.

"Part Two: Stories" is entirely fictional. Not one of the names, characters, or particulars depict or allude to anyone I know or have ever known, living or dead. Any speculation that the author is trying to reflect a certain individual would be truly unfortunate.

PART ONE
REFLECTIONS

Out-of-Town Kollel

YOU PUT ONE FINGER ON ST. LOUIS, another on Denver, pull them together, and on a standard twenty-inch map of the United States, you're about a thumb's-breadth southwest of Omaha.

If you're coming from St. Louis, the drive is pretty straight. You take the I-70 until Kansas City. There you switch for the 59A, and at Council Bluffs, before you cross the state border into Nebraska, you get onto the I-80 West. Once you're on that, you have about an hour until you see the white-on-blue sign standing in the middle of the divider that says: "WELCOME TO OMAHA (Est. 1854) — Population 335,719 — P. J. Morgan, Mayor." Then you're about two miles from the city center.

Omaha's Jewish population is listed at 6,500. Years back there had been much Jewish activity, but today Jewish existence is limited to a handful of institutions. There is a Reform and a Conservative temple, both of them large, stone structures built at the turn of the century, each with close to a thousand seats, and for the most part attended twice a year. And then there is a *frum* shul called Ahavas Achim.

Ahavas Achim was established in a storefront in 1915 by a few dozen established immigrants. The shul made Omaha a viable option for *shomer Shabbos* families in the breadbasket, and, with an expanded membership, they built their new shul in 1923.

In the front, there are wide stairs, four heavy doors, and a large, marble-covered lobby that leads to the shul. On each side of the lobby, there is a curved, cornerless staircase that leads up to the women's gallery and down to the small shul used for weekday davening, the large kiddush room, and the kitchen.

The shul itself is set up in rows of benches — three across and twenty down — with wide aisles between them. The *shtenders* are built into the backs of the benches, and bronze nameplates are tacked onto the seats.

The *bimah* is in the middle of the shul, three steps above floor level, with a latticework around it and on each corner, a column with a pole and a round light at the top.

Up front is the hand-carved, dark-colored, wooden *aron kodesh*. The rabbi's and president's seats are beside it to the right, and two flags are in a stand in the corner.

In the back, there are a few bookcases with siddurim — black Rubinstein prayer books with an old English translation on the facing pages — the standard Marcus-Berman *chumashim*, and a collection of odd Rosh HaShanah and Yom Kippur *machzorim* that have accumulated over the years.

The balcony upstairs has seats in three sections, all of which face the center of the shul in what resembles half a hexagon.

The walls in the small shul and kiddush room downstairs are covered almost entirely with "in memorial" plaques. You see names of Jewish servicemen killed in World War II, which stand out on their larger plaques with longer inscriptions, then some dates in the fifties but most in the mid- to late sixties.

The last rabbi of the shul, Rabbi Engelson, passed away in 1978, and the remains of his twice-weekly gemara *shiur* dwindled away. The president moved to Florida the following year, the vice-president passed away a year later, and, a couple of years after that, the secretary moved East to be with his kids in New York.

They have a minyan on Shabbos — twenty-five on *Shabbos mevarchim* — Monday, Thursday, and whenever someone has *yahrzeit*. But things are getting more difficult. When they have nine, they rely on the open *aron kodesh*. And when they have eight, they call old Mr. Eisig, and then rely on the *aron kodesh*.

The other Jewish services in Omaha are also fading away. The *basar kasher* butcher has finally sold out and retired. And Marty Cohen from Cohen's Jewish Memorials has been talking about moving to a more general line.

The statistics aren't encouraging. Intermarriage, conversion, and lack of affiliation are taking their toll on a dwindling Jewish population.

We are Jews. They are Jews. And we carry the responsibility to do something about it.

Perhaps we should consider moving out there and strengthening the community. The shul owns a furnished two-family house a few doors down. If it's not being used, maybe they'll let us stay there. I can talk to Max Kline, who runs the shul, and find out...

We could really change the whole community. We'll make the minyan thrive... We'll make a kiddush after davening that will attract young and old alike... We'll say *shiurim*, make *chavrusos*... We'll address topics in all areas from gemara to halachah, from *chumash* to *hashkafah*...contemporary issues, child-rearing... We'll make a Shabbos youth program and a Sunday program to teach the kids the basics of *Yiddishkeit*. We'll make Chanukah parties, Purim parties, sedarim on Pesach, sukkos on Sukkos...

We can live in the two-family house. Max said it's okay. It just happens that the house isn't being rented out, and the shul would be grateful if we'd come and live there.

They'll make everything ready. They'll kasher both kitchens. They'll make sure all the furniture is in tip-top shape. Each apartment, by the way, has seven full rooms, including a Hollywood kitchen and a study, and the appliances are brand new. The area is quiet and very safe.

Planes leave daily from JFK on Continental Airlines. Are you coming?

One second. Is moving out to the middle of nowhere the right thing to do? It is true that we all have an effect on our surroundings, but who says our surroundings don't have an effect on us? Out of town, without a Torah base, the outside influences are more subtle — and penetrate deeper.

We could keep it up for six months, a year, but after a while, the effect would be inevitable. When you pour hot water into cold water, it warms up the cold water, but the hot also becomes lukewarm in the process. If we become lukewarm, what are we going to be giving over? So, why go?

And what about *chinuch* for the children? Shouldn't that be taken into account?

Besides, is staying stronger in a Torah community doing less for the Jewish people? A Jew learning Torah in Brooklyn, New York, strengthens the level of commitment of a traditional Jew in Brookline, Massachusetts. A Jew doing *ma'asim tovim* in Lakewood, New Jersey gives the assimilated Jew in Woodlake, Wisconsin the determination not to marry a non-Jew.

Yet if a Jew learning Torah in a Torah community does in fact have an effect on Jews in a community without one, how much more of an effect he would have if he were learning in that other city itself. And if he were going with other families in the form of a *kollel*, the surroundings wouldn't necessarily have an effect on him.

Admittedly, moving to Omaha would be a very big and challenging move. But how about Albany — Jewish population: 10,000. It has a *frum* community and two established shuls — but it doesn't have a Torah base. There is a *mikveh*, a Torah U'Mesorah day school, *shiurim* — but Shabbos observance is considered to be a substantial commitment.

If a *kollel* would come, being *shomer Shabbos* wouldn't be an extreme, and *shomer Shabbos* people wouldn't feel a pull towards the center. The needs of the *kollel* families themselves would create change.

There would be inconveniences. Buying a *lulav* and *esrog* of your choice means a full-day trip to New York. *Glatt kosher* meat and *chalav Yisrael* can be ordered, but that requires a lot of storage space for freezing. Buying a *sefer* means having it shipped via UPS.

It would mean asking *shailos*. The main shul doesn't offer yeshiva-style davening. Do you start your own minyan and risk friction with the community, or should you daven there? Can an interested but not *shomer Shabbos* person be given an *aliyah*? And how is *shemiras Shabbos* measured?

But the interaction — the *chavrusos* developed, the

shiurim given, the Shabbos *ruach* extended to the community — would have a tremendous effect.

Perhaps we can't change the world. But ten of us could change Albany.

Vintage Thought

WE CHANGE AS WE GET OLDER. Situations change, needs change, and *we* change to adapt to them. Our concerns become more general: that we are well, that the children are well, that there is food on the table, and that basic needs are being taken care of. And as time goes on, we begin to see things more clearly.

We pick up more as we age. We understand more, we know more: about living, about life, and about living life.

At fourteen you understand. But your base is very limited. You haven't experienced success. You haven't experienced failure. You haven't experienced making difficult decisions. And you haven't experienced living with their consequences.

When you reach twenty, you've seen a lot more. You've seen things go right, and you've seen things go wrong. You've seen personal needs, personal pursuits...and you've seen how they come up against communal needs and communal pursuits. You've seen people who are easy to deal with and people who are difficult. And you begin to get an understanding of the role money plays in life.

At fourteen, you think being tall and good-looking are the most important things in life. When you turn twenty, you realize how much more important intelligence, ability, and personality are. Your base has widened. You're seeing the same things you saw earlier — but you're seeing them through a wider lens.

It *is* widened at twenty. But it is widened only in this regard. In other areas it's still narrow.

At twenty you don't understand why parents spoil their children. "Don't they understand that all of the individual good they're giving is adding up to a negative total?" you wonder. But then a few years pass. You marry, have children of your own...and spoil them just the same. At twenty you just didn't understand what a child means to a parent.

I used to think that at thirty or thirty-five this ladder of understanding reaches its peak. By then, you should have reached a clear understanding — and should be able to live accordingly.

But it seems that this ladder never ends.

At forty, people will tell you they have a clearer understanding of things than they had at thirty-five. And at forty-five, they will tell you they have a clearer understanding than they had at forty.

At thirty you want your children to be perfect. At

forty you want them to be well accomplished. And at fifty you want them to be happy.

As you get older, you begin to realize that you cannot control the levels of accomplishment of your children. Of course, you can set them on the road. But what they will end up doing is mainly up to them.

That doesn't mean older people are more knowledgeable than younger people. A fourteen-year-old can be more knowledgeable than a forty-year-old.

It doesn't mean older people are smarter than younger people. Younger people can have sharper intellects than older people.

It means they understand more. Not *chachmah* — *binah*.

Perhaps older people have a clearer understanding than we do.

Shabbos

SHABBOS. It starts when the house begins to quiet down an hour-and-a-half before the *zeman*. The husband and son leave together and head for the *beis medrash* to learn *mesechtas Shabbos* as they do every Friday afternoon.

They daven *minchah* with the minyan that has gathered — a *minchah* that is much more special than those of the other days of the week.

As the sun begins to set, they welcome Shabbos HaMalkah with a joyous and uplifting *kabalas Shabbos*. They sing *"Lecha Dodi"* and daven a moving *ma'ariv* that stirs something inside them and leaves them feeling truly like another person — one with a *neshamah yeseirah*.

After *ma'ariv*, they wish the others a *"gut Shabbos"* and begin to make their way home. They walk with an easier, slower walk than usual, and they discuss the gemara they have just learned.

The house at which they arrive has been transformed.

It is clean and sparkling. The silver has been polished. The children's toys have been collected and put away, and the kitchen is now in order.

All the children are dressed in their finest clothes and have been eagerly awaiting their father's return.

The table is truly magnificent. The beautifully embroidered tablecloth enhances the fine silverware and china set on it. The homemade *challos* are under an elaborate *challah* cover, and the wine and *becher* sitting next to them give the room a special look.

The guests arrive, and the *seudah* can begin.

Everyone gathers around the table, and the children join as the father and the guests sing "Shalom Aleichem."

They all rise and the father makes Kiddush, proclaiming the sanctity of the day.

The *seudah* is one in which the parashah and other Torah subjects are discussed. The children say something they've learned in yeshiva.

It is a meal of joy and singing, and hours pass without notice.

Finally the meal comes to a close. They sing *"Shir HaMa'alos,"* and then recite the *bentching* over a cup of wine.

The guests remain after the meal for tea and cake and continue their Torah discussion. It is very late when the guests finally take their leave and head back to their homes.

The Shabbos day begins at seven o'clock, when the father and son leave for shul to learn the parashah before the eight o'clock minyan they will daven in...

Are we together?

Perhaps it seems this Shabbos is straight out of the imagination. The magical atmosphere is one that never seems to occur in real life. The transformation of the house is never so overpowering, and the kids do anything but sit nicely around the table.

But yet...while the dramatics may be impossible to create, technically speaking, Shabbos can really be a day that is elevated above the others. It can be a day that is the goal of our six days of work...a day that helps us remember there is a purpose to it all...and a day that gives us resolve and direction for the week to come. And alternatively, it can be a day on which we rest to prepare for the next six days of work.

All I can say is that when, *be'ezras Hashem*, I will make a Shabbos of my own, *this* will be the Shabbos I will make.

A Time to Think

*T*ONIGHT I TURNED TWENTY YEARS OLD. And, you know, it kind of hit me: twenty years is a long time. It means two full decades have already passed...

Twenty. Third-year *beis medrash.* On the one hand, it feels like we were always here. On the other, it wasn't so long ago when I was in high school and even in elementary school. When those years come back to mind, it feels as if it were only yesterday that I was there...

Different memories come to mind.

Eighth-grade graduation, as we walked down the aisle and onto the stage to receive our diplomas...

A seventh-grade Chanukah play we put on for the class...

Some Pirchei trips also come slowly to mind — one to the National Mint, another to the Benjamin Franklin Museum...

The scene of a hurricane one afternoon in third grade

is also surfacing...

And then in first grade...going into class for the first time...

Going back even further, there is a vague memory of winning a fire truck in pre-1A, and another time a box of crayons...

But *snap*, and here I am, fifteen years later. In one second, it seems, so much time has passed...

I must say that I am satisfied to have reached this stage. I am not ready — if it were possible — to go through eight years of elementary school and four years of high school again.

This is where I want to be.

Yet I can't help but wonder a bit what these next twenty years will have in store. These are the years in which I hope to marry, raise a family, and accomplish as much as I can as a *ben Torah*.

There is a sense of responsibility, or more accurately, a sense of *lia*bility that I suddenly feel, not to let these next twenty years slip by without having something to show for every bit of the time.

Because if the years just quietly slip by, what will I have then...except twice as many memories?

Whole Lives

*T*HE ARGUMENT CAME FROM A MAN in his late thirties wearing a brown tweed jacket and gray pants, sporting a trimmed red beard and carrying his tallis and tefillin.

"You can't live your life *halb* in and *halb* out," he argued. "It doesn't go. You either learn or you work. If you're learning, great. But some of us have got to work. And when we do, we've got to be able to work. We can't wake up at five-thirty in the morning to go to a *daf yomi shiur* and then drain all our *kochos* from the rest of the day.

"When I retire, *be'ezras Hashem*, I'm going to sell my business and sit and learn *vi ess darft tzu zein* [the way it should be done], believe me. But until then, we've got to work *vi ess darft tzu zein*, too..."

The argument was a reasonable one. And *nu*, in a white shirt and black pants, holding a Paper Mate pen, I've been trying to write some sort of response.

You don't mind if I begin with a story...

My grandmother had an older brother Sheldon — the oldest in her family. His wife's name was Basyah or Batsheva — I forget which one — but commonly she was called Bessie.

Aunt Bessie and Uncle Sheldon were first-generation Americans. You know what I mean: They were the little kids in all those pictures of immigrant families standing on the boats next to their big leather valises or waiting to be processed at Ellis Island. Their parents were the ones who worked twelve-hour days for a weekly salary totaling in the single digits and who lived in tiny, over-crowded apartments in the South Bronx.

The kids went to public school in the morning, and they had a *melamed* in the afternoon for Chumash and a little bit of Gemara. But school for them was a passing thing. At fourteen or fifteen, they joined the work force to help out their families.

Even when they married they had to struggle to make ends meet. Life wasn't easy. But they saw advancement on the way. Their *children* were going to have things better. They spared no effort or expense in seeing to it that their "son the doctor" and "daughter the lawyer" went to the finest universities.

I never really knew my aunt and uncle. They were both a good deal older than my grandparents and passed away when I was still young. But I've heard they were very fine people. Very fine, and — it is always added — very unique.

Aunt Bessie and Uncle Sheldon owned a laundromat/dry cleaners. As you can well imagine, they were never really "in the chips." But even when they did have money, they would make every effort to avoid spending it. They would make a purchase only after it had been thoroughly established that the item in question could not be done without, and that it was impossible to buy elsewhere for a lower price. Then, and only then, would they go to the bank to withdraw the amount of money needed to purchase the item.

But they weren't just pinching pennies out of a miserly habit. They were saving for a goal. They were saving for their retirement, for the day they wouldn't have to scrub laundry anymore...

That day did come some thirty years ago, and when it did, they changed their way of life. They sold their little business, their store, their house, and from then on, money stopped being an object. They rented a penthouse apartment in a luxurious apartment building. They furnished it to meet their tastes. They started eating fancy foods and buying expensive clothes. And their days were spent doing anything and everything their hearts had ever desired — be it touring the Grand Canyon or just relaxing in Florida.

They lived like this for quite a few years, and lived to spend almost every penny they had saved during all those difficult times.

When I first heard about their lifestyle, I saw it as

admirable. Not for *what* they did; I didn't see anything special about spending their retirement years just eating good food and dressing in fine clothes. It was, rather, their common sense that intrigued me. So many people live their entire lives with frugality, always saving and saving for the future, never realizing that the future has already arrived. So many people live with deprivation in the name of not spending, and then pass away with all their money in the bank. I admired my great-aunt and -uncle for having the common sense to use the money they had saved for so many years.

But you know, the more I thought about it, the more things seemed different. Somehow, for people with their values, I wasn't so certain they had done the right thing. The idea of living a life of deprivation to facilitate living lavishly in the years of retirement is something I find very questionable. Time is something that can't be made up. Ten years of luxury does nothing to take away from the deprivation of forty-five years. You end up with ten years of lavishness — and forty-five years of deprivation. It seems a lot smarter to live an entire life as best you can, rather than deprive yourself of everything above the necessities to finance luxuries later on in life.

Getting back to the man's argument. Learning full-time later on in life? It's a great idea. But those years later won't make up for these years now. Whatever we learn during these years is what is going to be counted for these years. Surely it is smarter to spend our *entire* lives as well and as productively as we can.

The Ups and the Downs

BENNY NUSSBAUM IS AN OLD FRIEND of Mordechai and Shany Kaufler, and Mordy and Shany are my aunt and uncle. So when their youngest daughter got married Tuesday night, we were both there.

My aunt and uncle had asked the cousins to come early for a big portrait of the family, so we Wolfson boys davened the first *ma'ariv* — around 5:40 — on that mid-November night and, together with my parents and sisters, drove over in the family station wagon. But, as we should have expected, things were behind schedule, so it was decided that we'd take the picture *after* the *chuppah*, together with both the *chasan* and *kallah*.

It was still early, and most of the guests hadn't yet arrived. It was only us: the families on both sides, a few great-uncles and -aunts, and Benny and his wife.

The band was setting up in the smorgasbord room, where the families were all congregated, running lines from the outlets and taping them to the floor. I decided to go to the *chasan*'s room. The *chasan* was there with his father and brothers, standing next to the head of a long table covered with food and talking jokingly with one of his relatives. I didn't know any of them — not the *chasan*, his father, his brothers, or his relative — and...well, I guess it's never the same when you're at a *chasunah* as cousin of the *kallah*. It's just not so comfortable, if you know what I mean. So I sat down in the middle of the table and took a piece of chocolate cake.

The *rav* of their shul came in, and the *chasan* and his father sat down with him. My uncle came in, too — although he didn't sit down — and a few others trickled in.

Then Benny entered, and by the way he looked over the table and then sat down in the middle opposite me, it was obvious that he, too, didn't feel so... I guess you know what I mean.

Benny and I have met before. We meet at all the Kaufler *simchahs*.

"*Mazel tov, mazel tov!*" he said. "You're... One second, I'll tell you who you are."

He drummed his fingers on the table, and then he remembered.

"You're Mordy's nephew — Shany's sister's son. Isn't that right?"

"That's right," I replied.

"Last time we met must have been at Yehoshua's bar

mitzvah five years ago," he said. "But you couldn't have been more than fifteen or sixteen at the time."

I nodded. That was about right.

"How old are you now?" he asked.

"I'll be twenty-one in a month."

"Very nice..."

He took a piece of plain sponge cake. The room was starting to fill up. A few neighbors and relatives came in and sat near the front.

Benny took another piece of cake and poured a glass of soda. "Yeah, twenty-one is a good year," he said, then he pulled off the top of the piece of cake, toyed with it for a few seconds, and ate it.

I wasn't sure what he was trying to say.

"I was just thinking... You don't mind if I think aloud, do you?"

I shook my head. "Not at all."

He took off the bottom of the piece of cake and ate that, too.

"You know," he said with a soft laugh, "life is ups, and life is downs.

"I mean, you start off in the first grade, all the way on the bottom. That's how it is. The school is full of such big guys, and you feel so small. Then for seven years you slowly get bigger and bigger, until finally, after all that time, you've made it to the top. You're in the eighth grade — one of the oldest guys in the school."

He broke the rest of the piece of cake in half and ate part of it.

"Then the year passes, and you're in the ninth grade — right back on the bottom again. You're now in the youngest *shiur* of the *mesivta.*"

The room was filling up even more. A vanload of the *chasan*'s friends came in, and our conversation drifted off. My uncle sat down at the front, and Benny went to sit next to him.

Things began to move. The *tenaim* were read, and the *chasan* was danced to the *badeken* and then to the pre-*chuppah* room.

The men began to daven *ma'ariv*. Since I had already davened, I went into the *chuppah* room and took a seat in the middle, near the aisle on the right.

The *chasan*'s younger brothers were busy in the front testing the mike and making sure it stayed at the right height, and the friend who was going to be singing was over on the side finding the right key.

Other people began coming in. A couple of older men, some young kids, and then Benny with his wife. She went over to the left, and Benny turned to the right. He noticed me, gave a little wave, and came over.

"Sorry about before," he apologized as he sat down in the chair next to me. "I had to go over to Mordy."

"Oh, no problem," I answered a bit uneasily.

People were entering, walking slowly and talking,

and the mood slowed down a bit.

"Where are you learning, again?" he asked.

"Somerset."

"That's right. You told me last time."

Then he remembered.

"Oh, we were in the middle of something. About the ups and the downs... Yeah," he said with a laugh. "You finally get up to eighth grade, and then before you know it, you're in ninth grade, on the bottom again. Three years later you're on the top, then the next year you're in first-year *beis medrash* — the youngest *shiur*.

"Then," he added, "you go up again. At twenty-one you're really at the top. You're already in the highest *shiur*, the younger guys look up to you, you're deciding things in the yeshiva, and people are beginning to suggest *shidduchim* to you. Everything is great.

"In the right time, of course, you find the right one, get married, have your first kid, and you just couldn't have asked for more.

"But then," he continued, "time moves on again. You have a second, then a third child. And you're just one more *kollel* man. No one is particularly looking up to you; no one is specifically asking you how to run things. You're having a tough time making ends meet, and no one's volunteering to do it for you. It's downright difficult.

"I guess that's the way it goes," he said, laughing

half-seriously. "Yep. I guess that's the way it goes."

"*Nu*, so which *mesechta* are you learning in yeshiva?"

And our conversation took a different turn.

We went home after *sheva berachos*. A few distant relatives came with us, and the family wagon pulled out full to capacity.

Sometimes I wonder. Was what Benny said true? Is that actually how things go? It does make sense. And looking back, it kind of works out.

Yet, true as it may be, what is to be gained by this knowledge? It was an observation, certainly. But what is the insight?

Perhaps the best thing would be for us just to understand the idea — to make it a part of the way we see things. Not to look at the up years as individual ups, or at the down years as individual downs. Not to let ourselves get carried away by the up years and think it's going to be that way forever, or by the down years and think it's going to be *that* way forever. But rather, to see things in a larger light, and to maintain the understanding that things will always be easier eventually.

Just to have a clearer, larger understanding of the way life goes...

The Strength to Change

WE GET AN "OFF SHABBOS" every Shabbos Chanukah. The yeshiva arranges a bus that leaves for Brooklyn
early Friday morning and heads back on Sunday night.
But my brother's bar mitzvah was Sunday evening, so I
had to catch a ride back the next morning.

For some reason, the regular rides weren't available, but
finally I arranged a ride with one Avi Greenbaum — an
accountant who works in a firm not far from the yeshiva.

I got to his house with a couple minutes to spare, and
soon enough we were *coasting* along the Belt Parkway
heading for the Verrazano Bridge, which would eventually lead us to New Jersey.

After a few years of getting rides like this, you begin
to note patterns. Some drivers prefer a quiet ride, some
like to listen to a *shiur* or to music, and still others will
keep up a simple conversation.

This ride turned out to be choice D: none of the
above.

I was sitting in the front passenger seat, with no one else in the car. That's probably why Avi felt comfortable sharing his thoughts with me.

"You know," he began, sipping a coffee he had brought along with him, "sometimes you can't see yourself doing what a friend of yours has done, but just the same...you kind of admire him for doing it."

I didn't know what he was driving at, and he sensed it.

"I'll tell you what I mean," he explained. "I have a friend Abe — a super guy. We were together from ninth grade right on through college. And we were buddy-buddy all the way.

"But you know how things go. After we graduated from Brooklyn College and got our CPAs, things changed. We were hired by different firms, and we married and settled in different neighborhoods. It was very difficult for us to keep up the same kind of relationship we used to have."

We had crossed the bridge and were waiting to pay the toll and progress into Staten Island.

"Well, we graduated some time ago. In June, it'll be five years," he said, pausing as he threw two tokens into the automatic toll machine and returned to normal highway speed.

"A few weeks ago, I saw him at a wedding. And when you meet an old friend like that, the first thing you realize is how long you haven't been in serious contact.

We both decided that it had been too long. So we made up to get together the following Sunday — he and Sarah, his wife, would come over for lunch.

"Lunch was great, and I'll tell you, it was so much like the old days. Me and Abe, you know, sitting and talking…

"Anyway, after lunch our wives went out for a walk around the neighborhood, and we went into the living room. We talked a little, and then he said something so matter-of-factly it almost knocked me out of my easy chair.

" 'Oh, Avi,' he said. 'You know, I'm not working for Brockman and Stuart anymore…'

"I hadn't known. 'That's terrible,' I replied. 'Are they really doing so badly that they've had to lay people off?'

" 'No,' he said. 'They aren't doing badly at all.'

" 'Well, Abe, whatever the case may be,' I assured him, 'I'm going to do all I can to help you get another job. First thing tomorrow morning, I'm going to make inquiries to see what's available in my firm.'

"Abe hesitated. 'Avi,' he said, 'I left voluntarily.'

"Voluntarily? I couldn't believe it. Brockman and Stuart is a firm people do anything to get into. They pay great salaries, give unbelievable benefits, and offer significant pensions. And the job that he'd had was one with unlimited potential.

" 'Whatever for?' I asked.

"He waited a few seconds, trying to choose the right words. 'Avi, if there is one thing in the world I love, it's teaching kids. It's not something I can explain, but just the same, it's something I really enjoy. I've decided to go into teaching.'

" 'But you've put so much time into getting your CPA,' I said. 'All the hours we spent studying together, the three years of hard work, you can't give it up just like that.'

" 'I know I've put a lot into it,' he replied. 'But the fact that I've already spent a lot of time getting it is not a reason for me to spend my next thirty-five years using it.' "

Avi Greenbaum turned to me as he moved out of the left lane and let a car pass him.

"And that's what he's doing," he continued. "He's working for a Talmud Torah in Teaneck, teaching Hebrew grammar in the morning and English studies in the afternoon. He tells me he's never been happier.

"Personally," he added, "I would never have been able to do that — no matter how much I might have liked to. I just wouldn't have been able to give up everything I'd been working on for so long, just like that. And especially not a promising job like his.

"But by the same token, I kind of admire him. You know, the strength of character, the determination he had, to give up everything and make a move he wanted."

By now we were nearing Somerset and the yeshiva, so I started gathering my things together. We traveled the remainder of the ride in silence, and I thanked him as he pulled into the yeshiva parking lot. He drove off, and in no time he was lost in traffic on the busy intersection a few blocks away.

After taking a few seconds to clear my thoughts, I made my way to the dormitory to put my things away.

It was definitely strength of character that enabled his friend to change professions. That was clear. Yet if the difference in salary wasn't such an overriding factor, why shouldn't anyone else in his place do the same thing? What's done is done, I thought. But why should the future be dictated by the past?

The dorm building was locked, and I punched in the five-digit code. And you know, as I walked up the stairs, it suddenly occurred to me. How *could* anyone let the past be a reason to continue what he's doing now, and limit himself so much? How could the fact that someone has already put a lot of time into one thing be a reason to hold him back from doing another thing, one he feels he's better off doing?

There are so many people out there who want to change the direction of their lives. They want to take an early retirement and spend their time learning, or something like it. But the fact that they are already involved in something else, the fact that they have already invested time and effort into their professions, makes it more difficult for them to make the move.

Somehow, this is a strength we have to come up with. Because if we don't, what will our future hold besides more of what we've been doing until now?

What could it hold that is more significant?

The Pursuit of Fame

*W*E WERE SITTING DOWNSTAIRS in the dining room after *shacharis*, having breakfast: bread, milk, and hot cereal. We get scrambled eggs on Mondays and Thursdays, in which case we don't get hot cereal, and we get French toast every other Sunday. The yeshiva provides coffee in a big metal urn for the *bachurim* and for whoever passes by and wants a hot drink.

Two men entered the dining room and headed for the coffee urn. "So tell me, Shloima," one was saying to his friend trailing a few steps behind, their black and white hair putting them in their early forties. "I've got to be famous? I've got to be a big name that everybody knows? Whatever for? It's *hevel havalim.* That's what it is. It's empty. It isn't worth anything..."

He fished a Bic lighter and a pack of cigarettes out of his side pocket and pulled one out with his lips.

"Besides," he added, the unlit cigarette pinched in the corner of his mouth, "if I were famous, I'd have so many problems. I wouldn't have any privacy. Anything I'd do or say would be noticed and spoken about. *Baruch Hashem*, I'm not famous!"

Somehow it seemed this man wasn't so convinced of what he was saying. More probably, he would actually have loved to be famous. But because at middle age he was beginning to realize that it might not happen after all, he was taking a different approach.

When people who aren't famous talk about "how vain is fame," there is a basic perception that they're doing so because they haven't been able to make their own name a household word.

I am not famous, and my point is that fame is not worth pursuing.

So where do I begin?

Actually, there may be some subjectivity in my words. You see, at my age — twenty — there is no real internal pressure to become famous. None of my friends are famous. None of the people I went to yeshiva with are famous. And no one expects us to be.

So why should I feel challenged by fame?

To be honest, fame feels pretty good:

"Shhh, he's going to hear you."

"That's really him. I can't believe it!"

"Of course it is. Don't you recognize him?"

"Yes, but he looks so different!"

"Shhh, you're talking too loud. He's just wearing a differ-

ent pair of glasses, that's all."

"Wow! I can't believe this!"

"Shhh!"

But what is it about fame that attracts us? It seems there is something beneath the surface.

If you are famous and are the topic of conversation, you have become someone who is worth talking about. And if you have become someone worth talking about, you have become someone who is successful. So the desire for fame is a desire to be successful in life.

Yet fame in itself does not represent accomplishment. You can be famous for reasons that do not include success.

If you are asked to discuss a matter with the president of the United States, and then you hold a press conference with him afterwards, you will be famous even though there may be no change in policy at all. If something unique happens to you, you will be spoken about even if there was no accomplishment.

Fame is actually what gives us the *feeling* of accomplishment. It is this feeling that attracts us.

Just to be known by a lot of people, as are the local grocer and bus driver, is not attractive. It's being known in a way that implies accomplishment that draws us.

It seems, though, rather than spend our time and efforts pursuing fame and just *feeling* accomplished, it would be smarter and more productive for us to work harder in order to actually *be* accomplished.

The Desire to Own

*I*T WAS A SUNDAY, two or three days after Pesach, and it had been raining off and on all day.

Every so often, when I'm home from yeshiva, my grandparents invite me over for a lunch or a supper. The family goes over regularly, but since I'm usually away in yeshiva, we don't really see each other except for *simchahs*. So these meals arc a good opportunity for us to spend time together.

On my way home from my grandparents' afterwards, I was standing on the corner of Twelfth Avenue and Fiftieth Street, holding an umbrella and waiting for the bus. But no bus was in sight, and with the rain only a drizzle and the walk only twenty-five minutes, I decided to walk.

Anyway, as I was going down Fiftieth Street, the rain began to come down harder. Until then the umbrella had been holding its own, but now, with the rain falling more determinedly and the wind blowing in powerful gusts, we both needed a respite.

Across the street, on Thirteenth Avenue, there was a camera store with one of those large, black-on-red window signs that read: "Cash Crunch Sale — 20% Off Everything in Stock." So I figured I might as well go in and see what they had.

There weren't a lot of customers inside. There was a man in the front who obviously knew cameras discussing the capabilities of a flash with the store owner, and there was a lady in her fifties looking over one of those cameras that come in a bubbled package together with the batteries and film — no doubt for a grandchild. And then, well, suddenly there was me.

"Can I help you?" a young salesman offered.

"Oh, I'm just looking," I replied, suddenly feeling all too conspicuous.

"No problem," he said. "If you need help, come over and ask."

The regular prices seemed okay. And with the twenty percent off, they seemed good.

There were a lot of cameras, all different makes and models, each one with its own features. It seemed that perhaps I could use a salesman after all.

I explained what I was interested in: a sturdy camera with a zoom lens for about $170.

"Hey, Mike," the salesman called to the owner, who by then had gone to the back of the store. "What have we got in a zoom for one-seventy?"

The boss came out from behind the curtain and made his way over, staying behind the display counter that ran the length of the store.

"How are ya?" he said with a smile. "Hmm, so you're looking for a zoom for one-seventy," he said softly as he turned around and looked at the shelves. "We should have something."

He put a few cameras down on the counter — one, two, three — drummed his fingers on the shelf, and then turned around. Briefly he explained the features of each camera and said that they were all on sale for a hundred seventy-five.

There was another, more expensive-looking camera on the shelf that he hadn't taken down, and I asked him about it.

It was a Canon Sure Shot Z-85, with 35–85 zoom, three-point auto-focus, red-eye protection, date coding, water resistance, and a range of a thousand feet, he explained. But it was more expensive. On sale, it was two hundred dollars.

He took it down and showed it to me. He demonstrated how to open and close the shutter and how to use the zoom. I tried it a few times — from thirty-five all the way to eighty-five and back again — and then shut it and put it down on the counter.

He looked at me expectantly.

What now? I didn't have money on me, and I wasn't

ready to buy it anyway. I'd really just come in to get out of the rain.

"This is a real nice camera," I finally said. "How much longer is the sale on?"

"Up until Friday."

I thanked him and left.

The rain had slowed down, almost stopped, and I made it home uneventfully.

The camera stayed on my mind. It was nice, it was sturdy, and it had a big zoom lens. And I didn't have a camera. I called up two other stores to make sure the price was good (it was), and at ten o'clock the next morning I went back and picked it up.

Today the camera sits in my bottom drawer, beside the photo albums. From time to time I use it, but I guess I'm not a big picture taker. Do I regret buying it? I don't. It takes clear, sharp pictures, and the price was good.

But looking back...

When I bought the camera, why was I buying it? Not because I needed it. That's a given. I was buying it because I wanted it.

But why should I have wanted it? There wasn't any pressing need for it. What would be gained by having it?

It seems I wanted the camera because I wanted to *own* a camera. I wanted to own a camera with a lot of features and a zoom lens.

But why should I want to own one?

Perhaps it was because of a natural desire to own more. It seems that we want to own more — and to have more — because when we own more, we feel "larger." The more valuable and important the things we own are, the more "far-reaching" we feel. And I'll tell you how you can see this.

You're driving up Forty-sixth Street toward the higher numbers, and you come to the corner of Seventeenth Avenue. Just as you reach the corner, someone else does, too: a pedestrian your age, height, and weight, wanting to cross in front of you. Who goes first?

You've already stopped at the stop sign and can go ahead. But he has reached it the same second you have and can also go ahead. You can press the pedal so easily and in a second be on the next block. But he can cross the street and in just a few seconds, too, be on the other side.

You go four feet into the intersection, look left, then right, and drive through.

There is something very basic that makes you want to go first. You feel "larger" than the pedestrian standing at the corner. You're in a car — you have five-by-fifteen feet of property in your possession — and he doesn't. That's why you go first.

Ownership produces a feeling of "largeness." Not necessarily a feeling of importance, but of being broader, more extensive.

And that's why there is always a desire to own more.

Man-Made Meaning

*T*HE GRAYING, CHILDLESS DIGILIANOS live in a one-family house a few doors down from our own. As neighbors, they are the ideal: nice, quiet people who live their lives peacefully and privately.

When I was in elementary school, learning "in town," I'd see them quite often. Whenever we'd meet, we'd say hello and they'd smile. But basically that was as far as our relationship ever went.

They bought their house a while before we moved onto the block — around 1970 or so — and they paid very little for it. The previous owners had died; it had already been empty for a number of years without upkeep and the kids wanted to get it off their hands. These factors had a lot to do with the price they paid.

But over the years, they'd really done a lot to make it into a nice house. They had double oak doors in the front with white-painted, glass side windows, a wood-shingle, colonial exterior, and an elaborate garden they designed: short azaleas in the back and a neat double row of begonias beside the thick grass.

They aren't rich by anyone's standards. Frank — that's Mr. Digiliano — works in a nondescript job for the Transit Authority, and his wife, Clair, works in a local preschool. There isn't money to throw around, yet they manage to take care of the house.

They paint it annually, replace the shingles that break over the winter, and tend their garden regularly. Also, they do something with the house every summer. There is always some new project they want to work on.

One year, they spent the summer changing the windows — taking out the old, wood-framed, chain-linked windows and replacing them with double-pane Andersens. Another summer, they winterized their back deck, putting in a roof and walls that were removable for the summer. And another year, they took down their old cement porch and put up a new red-brick one with an expensive black, wrought-iron fence on top of it.

Building was what they found their purpose in. And they were open about why this was so.

"Building is life," Frank once said. "You start off with a pile of lumber, a can of paint, and some power tools, and you create something from them. You make something exist..."

And that was how things were.

But one summer something went wrong. They were busy building a new, air-conditioned study in the basement, and the way it was told, Frank had just run some new electrical lines when something shorted, and a fire broke out. It caught quickly on their collection of old paints, paneling, and spare lumber, and in no time the fire was eating away at the old wooden structure. They were able to get out, but by the time the first fire truck pulled up and began dousing the fire, their house had received serious structural damage. The fire marshal declared that it would have to be taken down.

As anticipated, they had a top-rate fire insurance policy, so the fire wasn't going to hurt them financially. In eight months, the insurance company paid, and the process of rebuilding began.

Half a dozen workers came with a tractor and tore down the shell, carting it away in big green containers. Frank took a year-long furlough, Clair gave up her job in the preschool, and they went out and hired a contractor. The construction began in the beginning of May, with Frank and Clair as hands-on architects.

Now if you're building new, it would seem that you would want to make changes in the layout. The wide front porch can be changed into a side one, giving you a larger living room; the side door can be moved down ten feet giving you a larger kitchen...

But it soon became obvious that Frank and his wife were having their new house built to the exact same dimensions as the old house. They had the workers put up the same Andersen windows, the same winterized deck in the back, and the same brick and fencing for the porch.

Things moved along, and it was just about a year and a half after the fire that Frank and Clair's house was standing once more — just as it had been before the fire.

Or at least that was how we looked at it. Frank and his wife didn't think so.

"You know," he said one afternoon when I met him in his garden doing some work, "the insurance company didn't give us back everything we lost in the fire."

"What do you mean?" I asked. "Didn't you have total coverage?"

"We did," he said. "And they certainly did give us back the money we lost in the fire. But you know, what the house *meant* to us...that they didn't give back. That they weren't able to do."

He leaned his rake and his clippers against the side of his house.

"We thought we'd be able to get it back by building the new house the same way our old one had been," he continued. "But it isn't the same. That old house was our lives. We would never have sold it. But this new one...it feels like a house we just bought a couple months ago. If someone offered us a good enough price, we'd sell it without question."

Their new house was an exact duplicate of the original. If their old house, with the colonial look, expensive doors, and red-brick porch, was important and meaningful in their eyes, why shouldn't this one be, too?

Yet he was saying that there was a difference.

You know, it's actually very simple. When he said their house meant so much to them, it wasn't because the house was truly meaningful. The house itself never had any meaning in it at all.

The things they had built — the sixteen windows and tracks, the ten-by-twelve deck, the wide front porch — had nothing inside them that was intrinsically meaningful. They were simply things that had been injected with meaning and were seen as purposeful because the Digilianos had built them with their own two hands — their own sweat and toil.

Objects? Meaningless. It's only what we bring to them — our efforts, our hopes — that gives them substance and worth. That's meaning.

Accomplishing
Accomplishments

*W*HEN GREGORY CAME TO WORK in the yeshiva camp it had already been on for a couple weeks. We start on Tu B'Tamuz and he came about Rosh Chodesh Av.

The yeshiva camp has about 180 *bachurim* — our whole yeshiva — as well as a dozen families of the *hanhalah* and the regular staff: half a dozen counselors, a couple of lifeguards, two canteen managers, the cook, and five waiters.

Besides that, there's the maintenance crew: three guys who clean out the rooms, mop the floors, and spend the rest of the day going over the camp with a nail-tipped broomstick and a black garbage bag.

When Gregory came on that hot summer day, with his sticker-covered knapsack, his rolled-up sleeping bag, and his distinct "Scut-tish" accent, he was coming for one of those jobs.

Gregory had a way of making himself known. He was a talker, and he got along with everyone pretty well. He spoke a lot about Scotland, his family over there, and his eventual plan to go back and work as a "*stuck*broker."

So what was he doing here in the Catskills, working a job that barely paid him the minimum wage?

One day, as he was cleaning the "rubbish" out of our room, I asked him. "Gregory, aren't you going to become a stockbroker in Scotland someday?"

"Thot's right," he replied with his Scottish candor.

"Well, if you could be a stockbroker in Scotland, why did you come here to...you know..."

"Why did I come here?" he repeated.

He put the head of his broom on the floor, one hand gripping the stick about chest high, and the other hand flat on his hip.

"Why did I come here, you ask? I'll tell you why. I came here for the same reason that I went to France, Italy, Belgium, Greece, and Egypt."

He leaned the broom against the wall and brushed some dirt off his faded Nike T-shirt.

"I want to see the world," he stated profoundly. "I'm young. I've got some years before I've got to start making a career, and I'm going to do it."

He sat down on the iron-framed bed next to mine.

"You know," he said with a philosophical expression on his face, "people go through their whole lives and have nothing to show for it. You ask the average old man in my place what he did with his life — where he went and what he saw — and what does he tell you? He says, 'I went to New York once, to Paris twice, and the rest of my life I was here in Scutland.' "

He pushed his shoulders back confidently. "I'm going to accomplish something with my life," he said.

Then he told me about the next steps in his plan. He was going around the world — west to east. First to Hawaii, then to Japan, and then to the rest of the Orient. After that, he was going to Istanbul, up through Russia, and back through Europe to England. In fact, he told me the goal of his whole life — to accomplish something by traveling the world.

The need to accomplish in life was the only force propelling him. He had no other reason.

He was traveling to accomplish. But why bother accomplishing at all? Was it for the good feeling he'd get when he looked back and saw what he had accomplished? A good feeling may be worth spending *some* time on — but so much time and so much effort?

We run into the same question in more conventional lines, too.

In many careers, from law to banking, from programming to accounting, people work ten hours a day, five-and-a-half days a week, to achieve a senior position in a firm. It's not just the larger salary they're after. It's the sense of accomplishment that comes with it that draws them.

But why accomplish?

Or from a different angle: Every year tens of thousands of people run the New York Marathon. They're doing it for only one reason: to overcome the challenge.

But why? Is it for that good feeling they get when they cross the finish line, and for all the congratulations people give them?

It's more than just that. Getting a good feeling — even a great feeling — isn't worth spending weeks and weeks building stamina and five, six, or seven hours running nonstop...

So what is it?

It seems that there is a desire to accomplish, not because there is any real reason to, but because if you aren't accomplishing something, you have no meaning in life. Without accomplishments, you are just waking up, working, eating, sleeping, and waking up again. And if there is really no reason to accomplish, other than in order not to feel meaningless, then the "accomplishments" are doing nothing besides filling that need.

Which, in itself, is not an accomplishment, nor is it true meaning.

There are accomplishments, however, which do have a reason to be worked towards: creative accomplishments. Building a house, for example, gives you a place to stay. Painting a painting gives you a finished painting.

But these accomplishments weren't done with the *goal* of accomplishment. You needed a house, so you built one. You wanted a painting, so you painted one. Accomplishing something wasn't the goal. It was only the end result.

Traveling around the world is a desire to *be accomplished*. Working hard to become a partner in a firm is a desire to *be accomplished*. Jogging a marathon is a desire to *be accomplished*.

But these things cannot be genuine accomplishments because there is no independent reason for their being done.

Torah, *avodah*, and *gemilus chasadim* are accomplishments done for their own sake. And they have an independent reason for being accomplished: we do them because they *are* the purpose and meaning of life.

And thus, they are *meaningful* accomplishments.

Why the Hat?

*W*HY SHOULD A *FRUM* PERSON WEAR A HAT? Why does it represent *Yiddishkeit*? In the past, men in Western society wore hats. But now most go bare-headed. Why should we keep them on?

Today, when meeting an important person, wearing a hat isn't only not done, it's improper. So why do we wear one during davening when we aren't talking to a mere person but to the *Melech Malchei hamelachim*?

Is it to create a barrier of dress between us and the nations around us? If so, why don't we wear the code of dress our ancestors wore thousands of years ago: a robe and a turban?

On a basic level, the hat is a Jewish way of dress because it is a more modest way of dress (see Rashi, *Sanhedrin* 74b). People did not wear hats in the past because it was in style. They wore them because hats were an expression of being subdued. It was an acknowledgment that they weren't able to do whatever they pleased, whenever they pleased, and an understanding that they had to act in a dignified and responsible manner. They didn't walk around with their heads uncovered, bare to the sky. The only people who didn't wear a hat were those who, as a result of a crude upbringing, lacked this sense.

It's only in the last decades that people have stopped feeling the need to wear hats. It's become perfectly fine to walk around with your head uncovered. You are allowed to do whatever you please, whenever you please.

But though society isn't bothered by its lowered standards, the hat still retains the modesty it inherently represents. It is simply a standard of dress that is more modest and, therefore, a Jewish way of dress.

But there is more to wearing a hat than modesty.

In the world in which we live, the new is always improved, and the old — more often than not — is seen as impractical. The contemporary is more sophisticated, and the older version is almost always more basic.

Life a century or two ago reflects this point. People lived simpler lives. They traveled less, didn't know as much as we know today, and couldn't do the things we do today. This lack of sophistication is often thought to have been the result of a lack of understanding and intellect.

The concept of fashion also expresses this point. New styles are meant to represent more than just change; they represent advancement. Last year's styles were nice, certainly. But they were nice for last year. This year needs something more, something better. This year needs something more "advanced."

It is to illustrate that the advancements of today in the technological, medical, and scientific worlds do not lend themselves to the world of Torah knowledge and values that I wear a hat.

Yiddishkeit is eternal. Our *mesorah* — our understanding of our role and obligation in *Yiddishkeit* — does not get more advanced. It lies established in the past by people who were greater than us, closer to the *hisgalus haShechinah*, and closer to *matan Torah*. The hat is a reminder that this is why we must look to them for guidance in *avodas Hashem* — and not try to plot a course on our own.

And even more.

Wearing the hat forces me to do the things my father and grandfather did — even if I myself do not know the reason for doing so. Certainly, I will try to find out the reasons. But the very fact that the generations before us did a particular thing is sufficient proof that there is a just and valid reason for our doing so.

So why not the robe and the turban? Because we are not trying to emulate the *gedolim* who lived a thousand years ago on an everyday level. We cannot begin to understand Rashi, the Rambam, or the Ramban. Therefore we cannot relate to their personal actions as an automatic guide in *avodas Hashem*. It is the *gedolim* of prewar Europe whom we can relate to, who show us which actions of the *gedolim* of many centuries ago we should try to emulate. It is to them we turn for direction.

So wearing a hat is not only a more modest code of dress. It represents the *mesorah* that we have — and continue to live by.

Mesorah in a Bottle

*T*HERE ARE DIFFERENCES IN THE LIVES OF PEOPLE who live with a *mesorah* — an understanding that they are following a direction that was established by people greater than them — and those who don't. This can be paralleled to the effect a cap has on a bottle of soda.

Have you ever seen a bottle of soda after it has fallen down a flight of stairs? The bottle has become rock-hard. Thousands of tiny air bubbles in the soda have been released and are now being confined in a very small area.

Yet if you would take the cap off that same hard bottle, things would change. All the compressed air would quickly escape. And the once rock-hard, non-compressible bottle would now become soft and squeezable. After a while, the soda would also change. Instead of being a refreshing, bubbly soft drink, it would taste like overly sweetened syrup. Also, without the cap, the soda wouldn't be able to survive another fall. One more fall, and the contents of the bottle would spill out.

Similarly, when someone lives with a *mesorah*, he is like a capped bottle of soda. The more persecuted and afflicted he is, the more he believes in what he does and the more persistently he will do it. But when he stops living with a *mesorah* above him, and he doesn't look to the generations before him for guidance, he has taken the "cap" off his *Yiddishkeit*. First all the fizz and zest will leave it. Then *Yiddishkeit* will slowly begin to taste different — not nearly as refreshing as it had been before. And if he gets knocked around and loses his footing (any sudden change), his *Yiddishkeit* is susceptible to spilling out all over the floor.

And this is why our *mesorah* is something vital for us to remember.

Expectations

RECENTLY I READ A SHORT WORK on Reb Chaim Ozer.

Reb Chaim Ozer was born in a small town in the province of Vilna called Ivye, where his father was *rav*. Even as a child, he showed signs of future greatness.

Once, when he was six years old, someone came in to ask his father a *shailah* on the kashrus of a chicken. Upon hearing the question, young Chaim Ozer answered it himself, basing his response on something he had previously learned with his father.

When he was nine years old, he delivered a difficult, complicated *shiur* to the laymen of the nearby town of Trob.

At twelve, he was accepted in the Aishishok *kibbutz* — a high-level *chabburah* of older *bachurim* — which included the Chafetz Chaim's son.

At his bar mitzvah, he apologized for not being able

to take out time to prepare a special *derashah,* but if the assemblage wished they could start any page of *Ketzos* or *Nesivus,* and he would finish it. This they did for several hours.

At fourteen, he was accepted in the Yeshiva of Volozhin, where he drew extensively from, and grew very close to, Reb Chaim Soloveitchik.

At nineteen, when he went to Vilna, he was invited to say a *shiur* in the Beis Knesses HaGadol.

At twenty-four, in a city renowned for its *gedolim,* he was appointed to his father-in-law's position on the Vilna *beis din* and effectively led the communal affairs of all the Jews in Vilna.

His *sefer, Achiezer,* expresses an encyclopedic knowledge. There is an absolute *bekiyus* in *Bavli, Yerushalmi,* and *Tosefta,* as well as in the entire scope of *rishonim* and *acharonim.*

Have you ever thought: Where do *we* stand in comparison? How far up the ladder do *we* reach?

Personally, I do not believe that I will *ever* know *Ketzos* and *Nesivus* by heart like he did at thirteen.

I am not convinced that I will *ever* be able to write a *sefer* with a tenth of the depth and profundity of *Achiezer.*

And I do not believe that I will ever in my entire life reach the level that he reached as a young man.

Yet we tell ourselves that we aren't *expected* to become what he became. He was a *gaon* — born in generations before us when people had greater capabilities.

Those were times when things were on a higher level. Those were times when laymen knew *Noda BiYehudah* by heart, when simple cobblers were able to quote verbatim from *Sha'agas Aryeh*.

Today, in Eretz Yisrael or in America, a fourteen-year-old is not expected to know *Nashim* and *Nezikin*, and a sixteen-year-old is not expected to know *Shas*. We are not expected to sleep three hours a night and keep awake by putting our feet in buckets of ice water. And even more: Doing these things, knowing so much at such a young age and sleeping the bare minimum needed to live, will not bring us where it brought them. It will not make us a Reb Chaim Ozer. We are supposed to do the best we can. If we do that, we can be assured that we have fulfilled our purpose.

Someone once gave an example to explain this:

"It works like a game of golf. Each generation has its specific handicap, and each individual has his specific handicap. The score you see is not what you end up with. You have your results, and then you have to subtract your handicap."

But you know, true as this *mashal* may be, there is one important difference. In golf, as you are playing, you're aware of the amount that will be deducted from your score at the end. And you can play confidently with that in mind. But in life, we have no idea of how much our "handicap" may be. And while it may be true that we aren't expected to reach the level of *gedolim* like Reb Chaim Ozer, any estimate of what is or is not expected is very risky to make. Because if it turns out that we were correct in our efforts, we will have lost nothing. But if more was expected of us — what will we do then?

Somehow we have to do as much as we can. We can assure ourselves that we aren't expected to do any more than that. But we can't afford to do any less.

Pedro's Lesson

THE MERIT SYSTEM ON THE WHOLE has proven to be most effective. You start off at the bottom, work hard, and slowly move up the corporate ladder.

Advancement for the custodians in our yeshiva also follows this plan. You start off at the bottom, working eight hours a day for $175 a week, and slowly work your way up. But the difference between the yeshiva's plan and most others is that, whereas normally your salary increases, in the yeshiva raises aren't in money — they're in title.

In six months, a hard-working, dedicated custodian moves up from simple "janitor" to more important "custodial engineer." Six months later — if he's still doing a satisfactory job — he becomes "indoor grounds-keeper." Another six months, and he's the "maintenance developer." And when he finishes his second year, he is named "executive manager of maintenance operations."

Nobody's stayed long enough to make it past that.

Except, of course, for Pedro.

Pedro is a fifty-year-old, Spanish-speaking, semi-legal immigrant from Cuba who got out about ten years ago.

From the first day he came to the yeshiva, there was something about him that was different. Somehow he spoke and acted as if he really could be doing something better and more important with his time. There was something about him that said this wasn't where he was supposed to be.

But just the same, things went on. Pedro fit into his job as if it had always been waiting for him, and, eventually, we began to look at him as part of the yeshiva.

One night I was going downstairs for supper when, on the first-floor landing, he called me over to an area he'd just mopped.

"Yu know, amigo," he said, "in Ku-ba, Ped-ero have moocho mooney. Ped-ero live in nice house. Ped-ero have fancy car.

"Den come Cas-tero — Fi-del Cas-tero — and de rev-lution. And he trows out Batista from power. Ped-ero looses every-sing. Ped-ero wanting to leave, but Cas-tero no gives visa. Finally Ped-ero coming to U-nited States."

This was going to be long.

"Listen, Pedro," I said. "I'd love to hear your life story, but how about another time? Right now is supper and —"

"*Uno* seconda," he said. "You get food. Ped-ero tells you some-sing.

"Ped-ero coming here, and Ped-ero have no-sing. Ped-ero have no mooney, and no one give Ped-ero mooney. What Ped-ero can do? Ped-ero already a man.

"Ped-ero no get training for new job. Why? Ped-ero tells you why. Ped-ero need moocho mooney to get training. And Ped-ero need good English to get job. And Ped-ero no have mooney and no have English."

I nodded.

"So what Ped-ero do?" he said. "Ped-ero doing dis. Ped-ero get food, Ped-ero get bed, and Ped-ero get *un poco* mooney.

"But Ped-ero have more," he said. "Ped-ero have happy. Ped-ero like what Ped-ero do.

"Yu know," he said, just as I decided that in exactly thirty seconds the conversation was going to end, "Ped-ero can do job two ways. Ped-ero can do job because Ped-ero need place to eat and place to sleep. And Ped-ero can do job because Ped-ero like doing. Ped-ero pick second way!

"Yu see," he explained, "when Ped-ero mopping floor, Ped-ero no tired. Ped-ero *love* mopping. Mopping is fun. Mopping is happy.

"*Now* you eat, amigo," he said, patting me on the back with a laugh. "Now you eat..."

And I certainly did. Most of the food was gone, but there were a few pieces of chicken left, and I scraped some rice from the bottom of one of the big pans.

What amazed me about Pedro was how he could get himself to enjoy doing something that all the other workers did with such disinterest. It sure is worth getting yourself to enjoy something you have to do anyway, I mused.

And you know, as I picked a fork and knife out of the boxes of plasticware, a connection surfaced.

When we learn Torah, we have to learn. This is what we are here for...what we are expected to do...and what we must do.

Yet if we must do it...why don't we do it out of enjoyment and out of internal desire?

If we work at it, we can learn to appreciate a piece of gemara...a *Tosafos*. If we keep it on our minds, we can get satisfaction out of a *Ramban*...a *Sefas Emes*.

And, you know, if we can do that, not only will our learning be more enjoyable and of better quality...we'll be able to go on and on. A little like Pedro.

The Small Time

*T*HE BEST TIME TO LEARN ABOUT COACH BUSES, I discovered, is when you're taking a long trip on one: something like the distance between New York and Detroit.

The front seats are probably the best. You can see out the windshield, and you get a sense of where the bus is going. But usually by the time you've gotten on, they're already taken or are reserved for older people.

The third and fourth rows are okay. But really there is little difference between being there and being in the middle of the bus. The seats in the back *aren't* good. You have to wait the longest to get off the bus, and the air conditioning is weakest there. But they do offer the sometimes-desirable advantage of being able to see everything that's going on in the bus.

The next-best option, then, depending on how the bus is set up, is to sit in one of the two seats right behind the rear door. There's no one sitting in front of you, and you get extra legroom and a clear line of vision.

Of those two, the aisle seat is the better one. It's always easier not to have to disturb someone when you stand up and walk around or take your bags down from the storage space above.

Anyway, the trip to Detroit is listed as twelve hours of driving time from when you pull out from the circular ramp at Port Authority until you reach the Greyhound terminal in downtown Detroit.

I guess you could say that those twelve hours were the sacrifice we'd have to make to get there.

You know how it is. The seats are never comfortable enough to fall asleep in, but the ride is so long and tiring that you really need the rest. Still, it's a lot cheaper than flying — and it's more dependable than walking.

Anyway, we were well into our trip — on the 80, twenty miles past Youngstown and about two hundred from Detroit — when a thought occurred to me...

Wouldn't it be great if someone would come up with a way to just skip all that time? The trip is exhausting, boring, and bothersome. Couldn't there be a way to bring us to where we had to go seemingly instantly, without awareness of the time the trip took?

Things would be so much easier. And things would seem so much more efficient.

Imagine: You get on the bus — now. You arrive — now. You do what you have to do. You come back to the bus station and you're back where you started from immediately.

If you're constantly doing things, rather than spending so much time being bored, you automatically do more. You think more productively. You become a person who acts more productively. And you don't leave things sitting around that aren't done.

If we had such an invention, we'd be able to use it for other purposes, too. Sitting in traffic, for example.

Wouldn't it be great if we could be home in an instant, with the press of a button, unaware of the time the trip took us? It would save us the bother of sitting around in go, no-go traffic.

If we could do the same thing to the time spent waiting for buses, trains, and planes...

But when you think about all the ramifications such a plan has, you see there is a bad side to it, too. If we just skip all that time, it will take away substantially from the time we have left.

We spend some seven years of our lives in cars. And we spend about three years waiting for buses, trains, and planes. Somehow ten years doesn't seem so easy to give up...

The things that could be accomplished in that lost time are enormous. Yet if that time is being wasted anyway, then what difference does it make?

The only way to give value to those ten years is by making them useful. Find things that can be done in a car: listen to *shiurim*, bring along something to learn, or even think in learning...

Capture the time.

The Chosen Nation

BETWEEN SEPTEMBER 1939 AND MID-APRIL 1945, Nazi Germany, with the help of its Polish and Ukrainian collaborators, barbarously slaughtered six million innocent Jews — men, women, and children — in what was later called the Holocaust. For those who survived it, and even for those who study it today, there are burning questions that will not go away, and challenges that refuse to go unanswered.

If we Jews are really God's chosen nation, how could He have let it happen? How could God have let those Nazi monsters murder six million of His people? How could He let 1.5 million of His very own children be murdered in cold blood?

I am not here to answer for God. The Almighty's ways are not — and do not have to be — understandable to man. However difficult it may be, we must remember that His ways are just, and that there was a reason for every single action perpetrated against our people during those dark years. What I will try to do however, is present the events that occurred during that time in a different light.

Date: 1930

Europe is teeming with Jews. In Poland, Jews constitute a significant 10 percent of the population, totaling well over three million. Western Russia, too, is the home of a very large population of Jews: as many as two million reside in the area from the western border to Moscow.

In Hungary, Budapest and its outlying areas alone contain over three hundred thousand Jews.

Germany, Austria, Rumania, Czechoslovakia, and France each have Jewish populations in the hundreds of thousands.

Now let us move the clock ahead twenty short years.

Date: 1950

The scarcity of Jews is eerie. Poland's Jewish population is down by 98 percent; the existing 2 percent are only there because they don't have the strength to move elsewhere. Western Russia has lost 1.5 million of its Jews.

In Hungary, Budapest and its vicinity contain less than one hundred thousand Jews — a third of the previous population.

Germany's, Austria's, and Rumania's Jewish populations are down 96 percent, 91 percent, and 75 percent respectively.

What happened in such a short time? The majority

of the Jews were murdered — murdered! — and the survivors refused to remain in the lands soaked with their brothers' blood.

Let us take a look at Nazi Germany — the empire that perpetrated this atrocity. The entire length of its existence was twelve years — from 1933 until 1945. It professed an ideology that defied the simplest logic: "*We* are the master race, and as such, we are entitled to conquer the world so it can serve us."

To this day, historians are at loss to explain how an entire nation — one which, at the time, had reached one of the highest levels of intellectual achievement — could support this idea.

For the first six years, Nazi Germany built itself into a massive force, then exploded into a destructive power that blitzkrieged its way through Europe, reaching the Atlantic in only three years. It maintained this near-total control of Europe for only two years, but during its occupation, was free to do as it pleased with the nations it had captured.

Germany chose to spend a great deal of this time, energy, and manpower murdering Europe's Jewish population — one that posed no risk to them at all. They did it with organized, well-planned operations: from houses to ghettos, then from ghettos to death camps. Nothing was done to stop it until the war was almost over.

In the civilized world, empires don't usually evolve

overnight. And countries don't just take over the world. They don't put exterminating an entire people highest on their list of priorities. And the nations of the world don't just let it happen. And right after murdering six million people, an empire doesn't just disintegrate into the nothingness from which it arose.

Such senseless, terrifyingly efficient killing of six million innocent men, women, and children of one particular nation — practically wiping it off an entire continent — could not have happened in the realm of natural matters. And it could *only* have happened to the chosen nation.

Reactions

*R*ABBI SAMUELS, OUR NINTH-GRADE REBBE, runs a *kiruv rechokim* project on the side. He works out of the Somerset Jewish elementary school and is in charge of the extracurricular activities for the upper grades. He takes the kids on *shabbatons* and Chol HaMoed trips, and he tries to expose them to a Torah atmosphere. He makes all the arrangements and finances most of the costs.

Twice a year, he makes a raffle. The main prize is the usual: a trip to Eretz Yisrael or one thousand dollars cash, and there are a few other donated prizes. The tickets sell for five dollars each, and the *bachurim* help him sell them over *bein hazemanim*.

We were going around our neighborhood trying to raise some money in sales, when we entered a big apartment building. On the first floor, we came to an apartment with a mezuzah on it — 1-C, with the name Howard Skelowicz penned on a piece of masking tape over the bell — so we rang it.

"What do you want?" an older voice challenged from behind the door.

"We're selling raffles for a *kiruv rechokim* project," my friend replied.

We were studied through the peephole, and a few seconds later several locks were unbolted and, still chained, the door opened a few inches.

"Who are you looking for?" he questioned.

"We're raising money. We're selling raffles for *kiruv rechokim*," I offered.

"What!?" he said, raising his voice. "I know what you're trying to do. You're trying to take my money. I know. Do you think I'm stupid?"

"We were just —" my friend tried to protest. But the man wasn't listening.

"Do you know that I worked hard for my money? And *you* want to just take it for nothing! You've got some nerve! I'm not going to give you a lousy dime! And don't ever come back to my apartment again!" he snarled, slamming his door shut and bolting all the different locks.

We just stood there. It had happened so fast that it took us a few seconds to comprehend. Slowly we walked away and headed down the hall.

Apartment 1-H also had a mezuzah on it, so we rang the bell. A man in his sixties opened the door and let us in.

"I heard the commotion," he whispered, closing his door behind us. "You're good boys, I know. Don't worry. Mr. Skelowicz has had a lot of *tzorres. Zul ess zein a kapparah* [It should be a *kapparah*]."

Then he told us Howard Skelowicz's story.

Chaim Skelowicz was nineteen in January 1940 when the Nazis entered his hometown of Melonka, a village sixty kilometers north of Krakow. The Jews of Melonka never made it to a ghetto. After two days in the courtyard of the local police station, they were shipped in cattle cars, two hundred people in each, in conditions inhumane even for animals, to that hell on earth otherwise known as Auschwitz.

He lost his elderly parents and two younger sisters in the initial selection, and four of his brothers perished during the three years he spent there. He lost his fifth and last brother three months before liberation in one of the last *zehl-appells* (roll calls).

After liberation, he was sent to a D.P. camp outside Warsaw, where he waited and waited to get the necessary visas and documents to emigrate to the United States — "*der guldener medina,*" as people called it — the land on the other side of the Atlantic. This was his only hope for a better future. In Europe he had no one. In America he didn't have anyone, either, but at least anti-Semitism wasn't in the blood of the people. Perhaps there he would be able to start anew.

After three-and-a-half years of waiting, he was

granted a visa. In July 1948, twenty-seven-year-old Chaim stepped off the Prince Freedom and onto American soil for the first time.

But he was soon to learn that it wasn't as *"gulden"* as people had promised it to be. There were multitudes of refugees looking for the same type of job he was — manual labor that didn't take much training. And whatever jobs existed were given to returning GIs.

He finally found a job in a factory screwing ballpoint pens together, ten hours a day for twelve dollars a week. It wasn't much, but it was a start, and considering the times, he felt himself fortunate. Four years later, he met his wife — also a survivor — and they married. They rented a tiny apartment on the East Side, and their life slowly began to take form. After three years of waiting, they were blessed with a daughter, Raizel, whom they named after his mother, of blessed memory. She was to be their only child, and they were grateful to the Almighty for her.

After ten years of work in the factory, Chaim — or Howard — got a promotion to a managerial position. With the added income, he and his wife began to dream of owning a house of their own. It took six years of saving, but they finally did it. They bought a nice brownstone in what was becoming a new *frum* community, Crown Heights. They put down a modest down payment and took out a mortgage for the rest.

Their daughter was growing up. She was already ten

years old and the apple of her parents' eye; it seemed that things were going to turn out well.

Then tragedy struck.

On a clear summer evening, while driving home from a weekend in the Pioneer, an oncoming pickup truck went out of control, plowed across the divider, and slammed into their car. The impact was horrifying. Their car went from 50 MPH to 0 MPH in forty-two feet. Howard's wife was killed instantly. He was thrown through the windshield and landed sixty feet away, breaking six ribs and his nose, fracturing his skull, and piercing a lung. Miraculously, his daughter, who had been sleeping in the back seat, emerged unscathed except for a few bruises.

Howard was rushed to a nearby hospital, where he spent the next four months waiting for his wounds to heal. His daughter was left in the care of neighbors.

It was difficult for him to get over the loss of his wife. Very difficult. But he managed — for the sake of his daughter. When he left the hospital, he was determined to put the pieces of their lives back together again.

But the factory he had worked in for the last sixteen years didn't want him back. They had hired a younger man to take his place and were very happy with him. "The workers like him better," Howard was told. All they could offer him was a spot on the assembly line — something he vowed he'd never do.

He had trouble making his mortgage payments. He

had taken the previous four payments out of his savings, but the account was quickly drying up. He finally was able to get another managerial position in a different factory, but it paid a lot less than his original job. It was, however, enough to live on, and he was forced to take it. Slowly he began to realize he'd never be able to keep the house.

He missed payments regularly, and when the bank realized he couldn't make them up, they foreclosed. The bank sold it for less than he had paid for it, and the prices had been going up. But as long as they got back their money, they were satisfied. Howard lost every cent he had put into it: the down payment and all the mortgage payments as well.

The four months he had been separated from his daughter created a barrier between them. They slowly drifted apart. She wasn't appreciative of what he gave her, and at times they hardly even spoke. He knew it had been a big blow for her to lose her mother. But it was a blow for him, too. Why couldn't she understand that?

He loved his daughter dearly; she was all he had left. "With time...," he reasoned. With time, she would surely realize how much he loved her, how much she meant to him.

But it never happened. Maybe he was overprotective and didn't give her enough freedom. But how could he? She was all he had left, and he was terribly afraid of losing her.

She rebelled. She came and went when she pleased, disregarding his demands, and then his pleas, for her to be more obedient.

Then she married a good-for-nothing — he did nothing but sit home all day, eating candy bars and smoking cigarettes.

"Don't do it," Howard had warned her. "The marriage will never last." He had tried to reason with her, but she was stubborn. Almost as stubborn as he was...

They got married in some shul out in Rochester. He didn't attend the wedding. And he didn't regret it, either.

They got divorced two years later. He had predicted it from the start, but now she refused to even talk to him. He would write to her, though, every few weeks, telling her that he wanted to patch up their differences and make amends. But she never responded.

And then, there was that bleak rainy day that destroyed his life. It was the day the mailman returned his last letter stamped "MOVED — LEFT NO FORWARDING ADDRESS." That was the straw that broke his back. Suddenly, it was as if it was the day of the accident again. Today he had lost everything: his wife, his job, and his daughter.

That was the story of Howard Skelowicz.

A person doesn't decide to be bitter. It is a reaction to tragic circumstances the person was unable to attribute to the cause that generates it.

Just as insecurity can be a reaction to being older and living alone, just as arrogance is often a reaction to feelings of inferiority and an attempt to gain self-respect by demanding it, so, too, bitterness and contempt for society is a reaction to tragic circumstances.

We may not be able to make people like Howard happy and jolly again. It may be too late. But we can try to understand where their bitterness comes from.

And we can be more thankful to the One Above for not putting *us* through such a difficult test.

A Time to Think — Again

*T*ONIGHT I TURNED TWENTY-ONE YEARS OLD.

It's hard to believe a full year has passed since I wrote that essay on how it felt to turn twenty.

Actually, twenty-one is only a step after twenty. Daily life is beginning to settle into familiar patterns. The Shabbos *keri'os* are becoming more and more familiar, and *selichos* and the *kinos* for Tishah B'Av are becoming easier and easier to read. And I am suddenly becoming conscious of how quickly and quietly time is passing...

At twenty, I felt like I'd stay twenty for "a nice couple of years," and then when I was good and ready I'd move on to twenty-one. But it's becoming obvious that time isn't waiting around for me. Before long, I'll be twenty-two, and then twenty-three.

Getting older, I'm beginning to understand, is not an option. It's inevitable.

To some, this fact may be discouraging. But truthfully, it does not have to be. I'll explain why.

Accomplishment for a *ben Torah* is only one thing: time spent in *avodas Hashem*. As such, if time did not pass, we wouldn't be able to accomplish anything. And even more: If time did not pass with the speed and continuity that it does, it would make the accomplishment of spending it correctly and purposefully all that much smaller.

And so, if at the completion of this year I will be able to look back and see it as being well spent, the fact that a year came and went will have been a gain...not a loss.

Planning Ahead:
An Exchange of Letters

DEAR BINYOMIN,

It was good to hear from you. It's really been a long time since I was in contact with anyone from our eighth-grade class.

So you're in an in-town yeshiva now. How does it compare to the out-of-town yeshiva you came from? I'm sure it's very different.

About when I plan on starting to train for a profession and in which area I hope to work...

I've started doing some serious thinking lately. You know, Binyomin, it's not just what I'm going to train in that I have to make a decision about. I have to decide what I want to do with my life. Surely, these are the years we "set the angle" that the rest of our lives will follow. A difference of one "degree" now, multiplied by sixty years, can lead us miles apart.

So the question I've spent the most time thinking about is what I want to do with my life — what I want to accomplish.

A couple of months ago, on a Shabbos afternoon, my brother and I visited the Jewish patients in the Park View Nursing Home. We were going through the rooms trying to give some life to the otherwise spiritless patients, but we weren't having much success.

On the second floor we noticed a room occupied by a man wearing a big yellow yarmulke, and we went inside.

We asked him the regular things: "How are you?" "What's new?" and "How's the food?" But after that, we ran out of things to talk about. So I decided to see if he could provide a topic of conversation.

"Where were you born?" I asked, sure that whichever country in Eastern Europe it was, it would lead to a story. But it turned out that he was born in Michigan, and lived in a farming town of some sort. Just the same, this gave him an opportunity to tell us the story of his life.

"I was born in a farming town in Michigan," he said. "We had a shul, a rabbi, and everything a Jew could need.

"Then I got married, moved to New York, and had a son. We lived in Bensonhurst, you know... Maybe you know my little *boychik*? His name is Sheldon — Sheldon Lerner — and he's a big-time architect in Piscataway.

"You know him? You do? You don't. Ah...

"He turned fifty-one just last month. He has two

wonderful children, and a beautiful grandchild. Yeah —
he's *ah zaida*! But she calls him 'Grandpa,' of course.

"Anyway," he said, getting back to his story, "I got
involved in importing, from Argentina and other countries in South America. I did that for forty-five years, it
was that long. And then I retired. I get Social Security.

"A couple of years ago I had a problem with the
circulation in my foot and I was in the hospital for
three-and-a-half months. Coney Island Hospital. And
now, here I am," he said, motioning to the room he
shared with his three roommates. "Park View Home.

"What do you learn in school?" he asked. "You learn
science? Biology? Chemistry? Physics? Yeah? *Gut*.
You've got to be educated."

Binyomin, what struck me after we left the nursing
home was that the man had told us his entire life story
in five minutes. That was his life — lock, stock, and
barrel. That was the grand sum, the total amount of his
entire life. *Five minutes*.

Binyomin, *whatever* I do, I don't want my life to be
worth five, or even ten minutes. I don't want to say, "I
grew up in Brooklyn and went to Yeshiva Toras Chaim
for elementary school. Then I went to Somerset for high
school. After that, I went to an in-town yeshiva and took
training at night. Then *ich hub chasana gehot* [I got
married], became a programmer, did that for forty-five
years, retired, and now, here I am — eighty-two years
old."

It's not like we have nine lives, you know. We have one. *Only one.* And I want to live mine as best I can. I'm sure you do as well.

I looked at the option of becoming an accountant. I've always liked math, so chances are I'd enjoy being one. But where will that leave me in the end? Where will I be *after* I climb the corporate ladder? I may indeed wind up with a six-digit salary and a senior position in a Big-Eight firm — but I'd also be planning my retirement, which would only be a few years off.

Law? Now that had me more interested. I'd make a lot of money right away. I'd work hard but take nice vacations and drive an expensive car. I'd basically live a very pleasant life. But...

Binyomin, there is one thing I *don't* want to do. And that is to spend my life solely as being part of a chain. Being someone who raises children only so his own children will be able to raise children. And in the end, so his children's children will be able to raise children of their own...

Certainly, raising a family of *b'nei Torah* is a great accomplishment. I don't debate that. But somehow for me... I don't see it as enough of an accomplishment in life; it leaves me with an empty feeling. Do you know what I mean, Binyomin?

I am not trying to downplay the need for *parnasah*. Every man has an obligation to support his family. But doing so doesn't have to take away from his ability to accomplish in life, the Torah way.

I'll tell you a story that explains this point well.

There was a *bachur* in Lakewood, years ago, who really wasn't *matzliach* in learning. Not a little bit. Nothing.

Anyway, he was getting older and his father, seeing that he wasn't accomplishing in yeshiva, wanted him to join his business. But the son was adamant. He insisted on staying in yeshiva. So his father went to Reb Yaacov Kamenetsky, who knew them well, and pleaded his case.

The following day, Reb Yaacov asked that the *bachur* come to his house. When he arrived, Reb Yaacov put his arm around the young man's shoulders.

"*Mein tayereh bachur,*" he said softly, "I spoke to your father. And I agree with him. Who says that you have to be the Reb Chaim in *lamdus*? Who says that you have to be the Reb Chaim Ozer in *pilpul*? You can be the Reb Chaim in *chesed*; the Reb Chaim Ozer in *ma'asim tovim*."

What I'm trying to bring out is that although the best thing most people can do is sit and learn, there are other ways to accomplish in life. A person can make a *parnasah* and accomplish by being *kove'a ittim laTorah* and by supporting *mosdos* and *chesed*.

As a matter of fact, when I first heard this story, I considered becoming a lawyer and spending all — literally all — my free time learning and doing *chasadim*. It would be like having the best of both worlds. And besides, there is even an advantage to this. I'd be able to do so many *chasadim* that I wouldn't have had the chance to do, had I been sitting and learning in *kollel* or working as a rebbe in *chinuch*.

Yet the more I thought about it, the more I changed my mind. This *is* my only chance at life, you know. If I had, let's say, three chances, I'd spend one of my lives living a comfortable life — giving lots of *tzedakah* and learning a lot as well. But I want to do more than that with my only chance. I want to spend my "nine-to-five" accomplishing as well.

I want a field that also produces basic employment. Besides sitting in *kollel*, the only *parnasos* I found complying with this are *chinuch, rabbanus,* and *kiruv*. So it looks like these are the areas I'm best off going into.

Will I be able to make it on the salary I'll get if and when I go into one of these things? We'll see. But I'm going to give it my best shot. My *very best* shot.

Binyomin, you're probably wondering why I'm thinking about my life as a whole. Why don't I just take things as they come?

I've asked myself the same question. And believe me, I'd rather not think so far ahead. It would be so much easier — so many less decisions to make. And besides, isn't that what most people do? Now you worry about yeshiva. When the time comes, you worry about *shidduchim*. Then, when you need a *parnasah*, you worry about a job. All without any specific direction in life.

But Binyomin, somehow I feel I'll get a lot further in

life, I'll accomplish a lot more, living *with* direction than I will living without it.

Do you know what people who live without direction end up doing? They look to their children to make up for what they haven't accomplished.

You always see people sparing no effort to produce model children. Be it in learning, in *middos*, in anything, they do all they can to help their children excel.

But doesn't it seem that in such a household, the parents are only worried about their children's *aliyah*, and have forgotten about their own?

Binyomin, that is not something I want to end up doing.

I once knew someone who, although he came from a very *chashuvah* family and many of his brothers were big *masmidim*, didn't learn a word himself.

"My brothers make up for me," he said. But I wonder. Do they? Somehow it seems that in this regard it's each man for himself.

How do you feel about this? Do let me know.

Your friend,

Naftali

Dear Naftali,

Hi! I just received your letter. Well, I wasn't expecting *that* for an answer to my simple question of what you plan on training for. But nonetheless, I appreciate the thoughtfulness of your reply.

Naftali, I must say that I admire your determination. Not many have as strong a will to spend their lives in the ideal manner you have expressed. But I also feel there are other considerations to be taken into account. Into *very serious* account.

Idealism, you must understand, is not something new. People have sought to live that way since long before you and I were around. And believe me, I'm all for it. It is, after all, something to remind us that there is more to life than the "hustle and bustle" of everyday living.

But we must also come to terms with the fact that unfortunately, life is not a picnic. Things do not always go the way we would like, and there are basic needs idealism doesn't provide.

Idealism doesn't put bread on the table. Idealism doesn't put a roof over your head. And idealism doesn't pay the dentist and pediatrician — or replace leaky faucets and burned-out electrical lines.

I have noted the reasons why I feel learning a viable trade should be a serious consideration.

1. You have to play the odds.

Naftali, we have to face reality. In all probability, we

won't get a job in *chinuch* that we'll be able to live on. So what's to be gained by spending so many years trying to get one? It's not like there is nothing to lose, you know. If we do try to get one, and don't succeed, we'll still need an immediate salary, and we won't be able to get the education and training necessary for a well-paying job.

You see people struggling financially their whole lives — always juggling more jobs than they can handle, just because they never had a chance to get proper training and enter a well-paying profession. If only they had spent a few years getting training before they got married, they could be working a lot less for two or three times the money.

2. The *frum* community needs *balebatim* as well.

Where will yeshivas get the support that they need so desperately if everyone is trying to become a rebbe? *Gemachim, hachnasas kallah* funds, *aniyim* in Eretz Yisrael — who is going to support them? Someone has to. And why shouldn't it be us?

3. We can "sit and learn" *after* we've acquired financial security.

Naftali, how well can you learn anyway, when you're constantly worrying about how you're going to pay for the food you'll be needing the coming Shabbos? How good a rebbe can you be when you're always thinking about how you're going to pay the rent?

4. It says in *Pirkei Avos,* "*Kol Torah she'ein imah melachah sofah beteilah.*" Any learning of Torah that doesn't have

work supporting it will end up disintegrating.

So we have to work as well. Well, once we're working, shouldn't we make a good job of it?

Again, Naftali, I am a great advocate of idealism. But I am also an advocate of realism. We can't just live in a dream world, thinking everything will go the way we'd like it to.

Awaiting your reply,

Your friend,

Binyomin

Dear Binyomin,

It was good to hear from you. I must agree that you brought up some good points, and I gave them considerable thought.

But somehow the reasons you mentioned don't apply to me as much as they might to someone else. I'll explain why.

1. "You have to play the odds."

Binyomin, I don't play the odds. Period. If it was something that wasn't so important, I'd certainly submit myself to them. But this is the most important decision I'll ever make: what I'll spend the rest of my life doing. I can't resign myself to something less ideal just because the odds are tough.

What I am saying is not unusual, considering what's at stake.

Take someone who decides to run for city council or state senate. The odds are always against him. Usually by ninety or ninety-five percent. But he really wants to win, so he resolves to beat the odds. He goes around knocking on doors and standing in supermarkets and gas stations, talking to people. He hangs up posters, hands out flyers, and makes speeches wherever he can. And he attends every single event and function in the community.

The odds are certainly against him. But they make him resolve to go the extra mile and *beat them*, rather than making him give up before he starts.

Getting a job in *chinuch, rabbanus,* or *kiruv* is definitely a lot easier than winning a tough election, I can assure you. And there is more at stake. I just can't give up without making an all-out effort.

And besides, getting such a job doesn't have to be so hard. True, in Brooklyn it may be tough. But Binyomin, there are enough places out there that need *rabbonim*. And with enough determination, I am confident that I'll be able to land one.

2. "The *frum* community needs *balebatim* as well."

Binyomin, certainly the *frum* community needs *balebatim*. They are essential to our existence. But my point is not that I feel there is something wrong with working. I don't. The point is that learning is so much better. And if I can be spending my time better and doing more, why should I — how *can* I — settle for less?

3. "We can 'sit and learn' *after* we've acquired financial security."

Binyomin, what happens if we never achieve that security? What do we do then? Besides, I can't rely on that argument for the same reason I don't use it regarding smoking. I don't smoke, even though I am confident that if I did, I'd have the self-control and ability to stop any time I wanted.

The reason that I don't is because I've seen so many other people make that same calculation, who are now helplessly addicted.

How can I rely on my ability to stop working after I "make my fortune," when there are so many people out there who thought they'd be able to and now, after amassing millions, are only after larger fortunes?

4. *"Kol Torah she'ein imah melachah sofah beteilah."*

Binyomin, if you go through *Pirkei Avos* in its entirety, you see one thing: Torah, Torah, Torah.

And yes, it also mentions the need for *parnasah*. But when it does, what it's referring to is the need to have a financial plan. You shouldn't just sit and learn without any idea where your income will come from.

But today, you can sit and learn in *kollel* for many years, with a budget — albeit a very tight one — planned out.

Binyomin, I must say I don't think everyone should be in *kollel* or in the *rabbanus* and *chinuch* worlds. I know people who are probably better off learning a trade and becoming professionals who support Torah institutions, rather than sitting and learning themselves. For them, sitting and learning would be like pulling teeth, and unfortunately, it would probably happen about as often.

And you know, even for people who *do* work, it doesn't have to take away from their ability to live a life of *avodas Hashem*.

Rav Hutner, *zt"l*, explained this point in a conversation with a *bachur* embarking on a career.

"Needless to say," he said, "I have never consented to someone living a life that sees employment and living a Torah lifestyle as two separate objectives. Your work and your *avodas Hashem* can be one, and they must be one.

"I remember," he explained, "when I visited Shaare Zedek Hospital in Yerushalayim, overhearing Dr. Wallach, *a"h*, asking a patient his mother's name so he could daven on his behalf before the operation.

"Tell me," Rav Hutner said, "is a doctor's davening for his patient anything but a life of *avodas Hashem*?"

So Binyomin, as long as they maintain direction in life, they aren't necessarily giving away their chance to accomplish.

But yet, it isn't them I'm considering now. It's myself. I don't want to accomplish a drop less in life than I can. And by not looking for a job in *chinuch* or *rabbanus* because it's "unrealistic," I may be doing just that.

Like I said earlier, it's so much easier to take things as they come. But that's what most people do. I want to accomplish more in life then they do. It's just that when I look at the alternative to idealism — living a life *without* direction and meaning — I realize that there is no alternative at all.

This, Binyomin, is how I truly feel.

Hoping to hear from you soon,

Your friend,

Naftali

Dear Naftali,

Would you mind if I showed your letters to my parents?

Your friend,

Binyomin

PART TWO
STORIES

Your Little Son

*Y*OUR LITTLE SON.

Just a few years ago you were a *bachur*, learning in yeshiva, and now... It's amazing how so much can happen in such a short amount of time. First the *shidduch*, then the engagement and the *chasunah*. And now, your pride and joy... Your adorable little son.

Your toddler son.

At two he's as mischievous as ever — emptying out everything and anything that isn't locked. He's also learned that if there's anything he really wants, he can get it just by crying a little. Of course, you know you shouldn't give in, but saying "no" is just so difficult.

Your cheder son.

At four-and-a-half he's in kindergarten. How much *nachas* you *shep* when you hear him saying the *aleph-beis* time and time again, and when he says something about the parashah at the Shabbos table...

Your growing son.

At six, he's in first grade. *"Meiner cheder yingel,"* you say when you hear him *chazaring* the Chumash he learned in yeshiva...

Your helpful son.

At ten he's as good as ever, helping with the house-work and taking care of his younger brothers and sisters. You're also beginning to notice that he's becoming an individual. His personality — what he's responding to and how he's responding to it — is beginning to develop.

Your bar-mitzvahed son.

Nothing can be compared to that feeling of pride you had when you heard him *leining* his bar-mitzvah parashah and then saying his *pshetl* at the *seudah.* Your son, the one you raised for the past thirteen years, is now halachically a man.

Your shtaiging son.

At fifteen he's learning in an out-of-town yeshiva. You watch with pride as he comes home for that one Shabbos a month and then as he picks up his tefillin, suit bag, and hatbox and sets off to yeshiva for another four weeks of learning.

Your maturing son.

At eighteen your son is truly an adult. Yes, the kids do become adults...it just takes some time.

Your married son.

Walking him down the aisle at the *chasunah,* there

was a feeling of overwhelming joy. All the work you put into him was worth it a hundred times over. Yes, your once-little son is now going to build a home of his own.

Back to us. I didn't really clarify who I was talking to —and I guess it would be appropriate to do so. You didn't think I was speaking to you, did you? Good. Because I was actually speaking to your parents — to your father and mother.

You were the cute little kid in the story, who by now has matured, married, and has a family of his own.

The same love and care we are giving our children, our own parents gave us...not too long ago.

Writing That Letter...

YOSSI PUT DOWN HIS PEN. Maybe this wasn't the best way, after all. Maybe someone else who knew more, who had more experience at such things, should be the one to do this... And besides, why should someone he hardly knew listen to his feelings about a matter that was totally personal?

He looked down at what he had written.

Dear George,

I don't mean to interfere with your personal life — and please don't take this the wrong way.

I'm not telling you what to do, it's just that

"Much too apologetic," he mumbled, as he crumpled it up and threw it into the garbage basket under the old, wooden desk he was working on.

Dear George, he started again.

What I want to tell you is simple, and it doesn't take much to understand how true it is. I believe it with all my heart, and I'm sure that if you think about it, you'll agree.

He crumpled up this paper, too, and tossed it along-side the other one. He was sounding like a missionary.

He sat a little deeper in his worn-out desk chair, taking a few minutes to organize his thoughts.

At last he began:

Dear George,

This is Yossi — your neighbor from down the block. George, while many things are better said than written, some are better written than said. And I feel that this is one of them. By writing, it will be easier both for me to express myself, and for you to listen.

I am writing in reference to your son Jason. George, I know how much you love him and want him to succeed. I have children of my own.

When we spoke last week you mentioned you're already saving towards his college education.

But George, when planning a child's future, you must remember that ninety percent of what a kid — and especially a teenager — does is a direct result of peer pressure. We are, to a large degree, a product of our surroundings.

When you enroll Jason in the kindergarten of P.S. 186, you must be aware that nine years down the line you're going to have one of the present eighth graders; and when he goes to Franklin High, four years later he will be one of the present twelfth graders.

Have you met them? You can see them every day at five after three, tromping home from school in packs of eight to ten. Obscenities flow from their mouths like water, and morality is lacking on the most basic levels.

George, how can you think Jason will stand out as the serious student you'd like him to be? How can you think he'll remain the "oddball," waving the banner of morality? In all probability, he's going to be exactly like one of them, from the crew cut with the four-inch tail in back to the three earrings in his left ear. You can only hope that between now and then tattoos don't come back "in" again.

You want a doctor. I know it would be nice. But you've got to be practical. You've got to be aware of how little studies mean to the kids in public schools. A substantial percentage of Jason's class won't even make it through high school. Jason will, I know. But what makes you think that when he does he'll be interested in more school?

You'll try to convince him. So what? When do you think one of those twelfth graders listened to his parents last? Fifth grade? Maybe.

It's not Jason. I know he's a good kid. But you've got to understand what happens to kids who go through the public school system.

Have you considered that Jason will probably marry a Jew only by chance? George, Jews consist of only two percent of the population. The odds aren't good. The possibility of having grandchildren running around with rosary beads and crosses around their necks is very, very, real. I can introduce you to my boss — he's a Jew with three Christian grandchildren.

But then again, a good deal of those twelfth graders will never marry in the first place, so there may not be grandchildren to worry about...

I am not trying to tell you what to do. I respect you more than that. I am merely presenting an alternative option. You can send him to yeshiva with my Michael. He'll be taught morals and family values. He'll receive a fine education, will definitely complete high school, and will be able to continue on to any college he chooses.

He'll raise a nice family — and in all probability he'll live right here in the neighborhood. And his kids will know their grandpa.

And, yes. He'll be a good observant Jew.

We aren't speaking about fanaticism. I, George, am not a fanatic. We're speaking about two basic concepts: One, believing in God. And two, believing that we are God's chosen nation, and as such were given the Torah to live by. Nothing more and nothing less.

Whatever you decide to do, George, please don't think I'm writing you this letter to "save my soul" or "speed up the deliverance of the Lord." I am simply writing to forewarn you of what seems to be a tragedy in the making.

Should you want to discuss the matter further, just

knock on my door.

I hope we can continue to be friendly neighbors.

Sincerely,

Yossi Kaufstein

The "George" in our story is our neighbor down the block. "Jason" is his five-year-old son. "P.S. 186" is the local public school. And "Yossi Kaufstein" is you and me.

And the letter...is asking to be written.

Buying Time

No MATTER HOW HE CUT IT, the numbers were always pretty much the same.

Yitzchak rested his head in his open palms for a second.

The piece of paper was already an unreadable jumble of numbers, percentages, long multiplication, and looping arrows — and it was only an hour after he'd started. He had told Miriam he was going to try to work on some new ideas, but he hadn't thought it would be so difficult.

He tore a new piece of paper out of a spiral notebook and put his pen on top of it. Then he went into the kitchen to make coffee. A heaping teaspoon of coffee, a leveled one of sugar, water from the kettle almost until the top, and then a little bit of milk.

The bulk of the budget was the few big items. The rent. Health insurance. The car. And baby-sitting. If one of these could be knocked off, or at least reduced considerably, it would make things so much easier.

They did have enough to survive on, it was true. But with the kids getting older and expenses always getting larger, things were getting tighter and tighter. Nickels, dimes, and quarters weren't counted. But dollars — single dollars — were playing all too much of a role in the weekly plans. And anything additional — a suit for himself, a dress for Miriam, new outfits for the kids — knocked off the whole budget.

He stirred the coffee with a spoon and carried it back on a saucer. They weren't going to borrow. That was something they had established long ago. Yes, if an emergency arose, they might, but *only* in an emergency. Once they started borrowing, there would be no end. They'd borrow again to pay it back. And then borrow again to pay back again. Somehow rolling loans always had a way of getting bigger and bigger, rolling faster and faster, until eventually, more often than not, they collapsed in a big heap of trouble.

So they were going to have to work on reducing the need.

Rent: $650.

He put it down in big letters at the top of the page. Then he went over the possibilities.

They could try to find a cheaper apartment. A $500 apartment would leave a monthly surplus of $150 — really a big help.

But in their area it would mean moving from a five-and-a-half-room apartment to a three-room one.

And the kids would have to sleep in a curtained-off section of the living/dining room. Now they had two full bedrooms, and everything fit in very well...

They could move to a cheaper area. A possibility. In the next neighborhood, they could get five rooms for five hundred dollars. But if they moved, they'd have transportation costs. It would mean a fifteen-minute ride every day to yeshiva — both there and back — gas, and wear and tear on the car. As it was, they were trying to cut down on driving.

And besides, it would mean an extra fifteen to twenty minutes a day to get the kids over to the baby-sitter. Where would the time come from? On Shabbos it would mean a half-hour walk each way to davening, in the winter and in the summer.

So the rent was on the page. Clear — on the top — and circled.

What was next?

Health insurance: $500.

Five hundred dollars a month — six thousand dollars a year — on insurance! Ridiculous! If they would only do something with that health-care reform they did so much talking about. All they did was talk and talk. When would they finally do something?

Tachlis. There were two options. (1) Having health insurance. (2) Not having it.

Without it, every childbirth would cost them $4,500. Doctor's visits for the kids, all twelve standard immunizations, checkups for him and Miriam — it would have to cost $1,000. And then they wouldn't have security. If someone, *chas veshalom*, needed a hospital stay, it would cost them $950 a day — $6,500 a week. A simple appendix removal cost $1,800 for the operation, and then there would be the days in the hospital.

So insurance was on the page, too. Five hundred dollars.

Baby-sitting: $450.

Terrible... Miri was making fifteen dollars an hour, and they were paying five for baby-sitting.

Maybe he'd learn at home. That's it. He and his *chavrusah* would borrow *shtenders* from the yeshiva, bring over their gemaras, and learn at home. He had plenty of reference material.

It wasn't practical. The kids would take up all his time. And wasn't the whole point for him to be learning all day?

Maybe they could find a cheaper baby-sitter. Perhaps. But the savings would be very small.

The coffee was cooling off, and he took a couple of long sips.

The car.

They had an '86 Buick with 92,000 miles on it. Wear and tear averaged $700 a year. Gas — they were trying to cut down on driving — $45 a month. And liability insurance — $900 a year. Could they manage without a car? Could they do it? Perhaps they could...

But it would mean big sacrifices. It would mean traveling in cabs, or having to ask other people for rides and conforming to their schedules.

It was an option. But it was a last option.

The rent. The insurance. Baby-sitting. And the car.

So they were right back where they'd started.

He finished his coffee.

So he would have to work on the other expenses. That's what he'd thought all along. Food was $220 a month. The phone bill was $65. Diapers were $50. And formula $45.

And then the *yamim tovim*, which when all was counted were $300 each. They'd have to cut down on each item as much as they could.

They'd have to buy their groceries only from the supermarket. And more chicken orders, less meat orders. No more disposable paperware — washing dishes didn't really cost them anything.

That was how they would have to do it. They'd have to count the dollars.

I was just thinking a bit. You know, if you're squeezing because there is no alternative, it is in fact difficult. Very difficult. But yet if you are cutting corners by choice: because by doing so you will be able to afford something else, then it's a lot easier.

For example: Let's say you want to buy a new dining-room set — six expensive chairs and a long oval table — and the only way you can afford it is by living on a tight budget for three months. Is cutting back during that time difficult? It doesn't seem so. Somehow the simple meals don't bother you; not being able to buy from the local grocery isn't a hinderance; washing the dishes isn't a bother. You have difficulties. But it is relatively easy because, through them, you are acquiring the dining-room set.

If we look at time spent learning Torah as an acquisition — something we possess and will always keep with us — and see the sacrifices we make as necessary to finance our purchase, it eases the struggle of making ends meet in *kollel*.

Competition

*T*ULLY LOOKED AT HIS WATCH AGAIN. There were forty minutes left. Or alternatively, in twenty minutes there would be twenty minutes left.

He had come a full hour early. He didn't have to — fifteen minutes would have been ample. But he liked the extra time. It gave him a better feel of the office before he went in. And it also gave him time to plan out his strategy.

There were four other salesmen in the room, all of them, no doubt, thinking up their own plans.

How ironic, he thought. All of them were in the same waiting room. All of them were trying to get the same contract. And each one of them was trying to come up with the reason why he would succeed...

Helms Hotel had decided to change the chairs in their hotel lounges, and had sent word for sofa manufacturers to make a twenty-minute pitch. Tully, a salesman for United Furniture Company, had been given the assignment.

The other men were fixing their ties, practicing gestures, trying to get the right spin on their presentations. He would have to do something different — something unique — something that would make him stand out.

He looked at his watch again.

The secretary called out a name, and a man in his sixties went in.

Tully had sat in the chair closest to the office, and he caught a glimpse of Howard Helms, the owner and purchaser, as the door opened. He was a heavyset man, with a mustache, an unlit cigar in the corner of his mouth, and no jacket. It wasn't going to be easy.

He could hear most of the conversation as it trickled through the door.

"...Like I was saying, we at McMallon Chair have been making chairs for years. Yep, chairs for years. A bit of a rhyme there, wouldn't you say, Mr. Helms? Might make a good motto someday.

"Anyway, My Grandpa Neil — like I was saying, my name is Norman, my father, may he rest in peace, was Frank, and my grandpa was Neil — came over from the Island, that's Ireland of course, in 1886 without a penny in his pocket. Not one single penny. But he came with a wonderful idea in his head. Chairs. He was going to make chairs. And that's exactly what he did. He started in a basement. My pops and his fifteen brothers and sisters lived on the ground floor, and the shop was in the basement. Grandpa Neil must have put in twenty,

twenty-two hours a day in the beginning...

"I still remember that first chair he made for my grandma. Now wasn't that a chair! Lion arms: wide, sturdy arms, so you could rest your entire arm on them, big, sturdy legs — all of first-class redwood, of course.

"And do you know what Grandpa added onto it? He added a rocker — a one-of-a-kind, detachable rocker — so Grandma could rock while she knitted all the kids' clothes until the wee hours of the morning. Now wasn't that nice?

"Ahem. So what I'm getting to, Mr. Helms, is that McMallon is truly a family enterprise. We put a hundred years of experience into every single chair. And everything we make is both supervised and inspected by one of the family. We aren't just a chair maker. We're a chair maker with a tradition. And we always say, 'Tra*dition* must be a con*dition*.' You like that, don't you?"

A few questions, the attaché case opened and closed, and the salesman walked out.

"Next."

A name was called. Time was passing. *Now* it was twenty minutes. Tully went over his plan. It was going to be different. Different, different, different, that was the key. And it was going to be short.

Another salesman came in carrying a big blue cushion and sat down opposite him.

Everyone was trying to be that one step ahead. Every single person. He was trying — thinking, contemplating, and planning — and just as he was, they were.

He listened carefully.

"...So right now you're probably asking yourself: Why should I pick Goodman Chairs? There are a lot of good chair makers, a lot of nice designs, and a lot of fine textures. Why ours?

"Well first of all, our chair, the Soft-Chair, equals any of the leading manufacturer's products in design, strength, and most of all, price. But there is one thing only *our* company does. And that is to service what we sell.

"Over time, there will always be wear and tear. A spring breaks here, a cushion is torn there, and the only way to fix them is by bringing the chair to a local repairman who charges you top dollar. We estimate that a hotel chain your size must spend two thousand dollars a year on such repairs every single year. And we don't think you should have to.

"We have a special repair department, headed by Mike — a wonderful guy and a father of two — that will come to you and fix the problem at cost price. We do it just to keep our customers satisfied."

A few questions.

The door opened and the salesman left. Tully's name was called. He took a deep breath and walked inside.

"Your name?"

"Tully."

"And who d'you represent?"

"United Furniture."

"So..."

The eyes studied him.

"Mr. Helms," he began, "I did come here to talk about chairs. But do you mind if I ask... That painting in your waiting room — that's one of Fredro's isn't it?"

"Yeah."

"Must have cost a pretty penny. Where did you pick it up? Lloyd's?"

"No, I got it in a shop in Manhattan."

"What does such a piece go for?"

"I paid twelve when I bought it four years ago, but now that he's died it's worth about double. So what's your pitch?"

"It's very simple," Tully began. "We've got a great chair. It's beautiful, it's comfortable, and the quality is great. And we guarantee a better price than anyone else. It's as simple as that."

"You have pictures of your product?"

Tully pulled the catalog out of his portfolio.

"The Elegance Seater is probably your best bet," Tully said as he handed over the catalog, pointing out which one it was.

"What do you want for the two hundred chairs?"

"Forty-eight G's."

"It's too much," Howard Helms snapped.

"We'll talk."

"You have a card?"

Tully pulled out his Pierre Cardin leather organizer and wrote down: "Tully, Elegance Seater, forty-eight G's, (212) 826-4800." Then he tore out the page and handed it over.

He couldn't just give a card. Everyone did that.

He thanked Mr. Helms, shook his hand, and left. The guy with the cushion went in after him.

Tully took the elevator down to the underground garage and walked to his car. Competition was so tough, he reflected, and there was so much of it. Everyone was trying to be a little smarter, a little ahead, a little better planned. If only there was another way...

But, he thought, the only alternative was communism, and that hadn't exactly worked any better. So he was going to have to keep on competing. It was going to be him. And it was going to be them.

That was how it was going to be.

But Tully was mistaken.

True, life is challenging because we have common needs and goals, and there aren't enough resources readily available for all of us. What we need, other people need. What we want, other people want. And what one of us gets, other people won't. So we are forced to compete. In yeshiva, in *shidduchim*, in getting a job — and especially in business.

But while it may be true that competition makes life challenging, in the overall challenge of life, things are different. Competition shouldn't play a role because each person's needs are different. You are challenged to bring out your potential. I am challenged to bring out mine. We aren't against each other, we're against ourselves. Other people's successes shouldn't threaten us, and our successes shouldn't threaten other people. The challenge is only what we are doing and how it compares to what we *could* be doing.

Big Doings

*A*HARON HELLER WAS MORE than just the foreman at the East Side based Klein Brothers Belt and Tie Company. He ran the ship.

Mr. Klein, Sr. started the business in the mid-fifties and ran it until he retired in the early eighties. He had intended his son Hershel to run it, but in the end, Hershel lived in Chicago and had properties to manage there. And so they'd hired Aharon to do it for them.

He was in charge of everything in the business. He arranged the import of ties from Italy and had belts shipped from South Korea. He arranged the distribution of merchandise to better men's-clothing stores in the tri-state area. And he was the one who made sure expenses were kept as low as possible.

He was being paid $950 a week. A nice salary, but nothing special. It was clear, though, that it was as far as he would ever go. There was no room for advancement.

But yet, for some reason this had never bothered him.

Maybe, he thought, it was his feeling of success when he made such big deals that kept him satisfied.

The way he'd get on the phone with the big manufacturers:

"This is Aaron from Klein's. Is Barry there?...Yeah, Barry? This is Aaron speaking. How are you?...Fine, fine, thank you. ...Yeah!...I know, I know...Listen, I need two thousand of your three-and-a-half-inch small-print collection...That's right. When will it be shipped?...Great. We'll pay in sixty...Very good. We'll talk."

And maybe it was the way the belt manufacturers kept on trying to solicit his business:

"This is a present for you, Mr. Heller, from Gerald LaMond of LaMond belt makers. We've been making exclusive men's belts since 1954. We hope you will place an order with us in the future."

Perhaps it was his sense of accomplishment at arranging tens of thousands of dollars of credit from the factories in Italy.

Perhaps it was a result of his power, the way he could hire and fire workers at his discretion.

But most of all, his satisfaction came from simply running the business, from making sure all the different elements needed to buy and distribute such large quantities of merchandise fell into place.

But lately, something was beginning to bother him. He wasn't benefitting from the money he brought into the business; his salary would continue to be the same.

He wasn't gaining anything when he opened up a new line of credit; his position wouldn't change.

How then, he wondered, could dealing with large amounts of money be a cause for satisfaction?

Large amounts of money made the deals more important, certainly. But how did they make the work more meaningful? If making a deal of *fifty* dollars wasn't a meaningful action, how was a deal of fifty *thousand* dollars?

Aharon Heller would go on running Mr. Klein's business. But somehow, his big business seemed just a little...smaller.

Actions are either meaningful or not meaningful. The value that is involved makes them seem more important. But it doesn't really make them meaningful.

That was the truth that Aharon Heller finally learned.

Accounting

GEDALIA STOLLMAN'S SALARY didn't cover much more than basic expenditures. It paid the mortgage, the car expenses, tuition for the kids, and health insurance, and it put bread on the table and milk in the fridge.

His *second* job, privately tutoring two high school students in the evenings, let them go beyond that. Six thousand dollars a year, above basic expenses, really went a long way.

When he thought about it, this second job let him and his family "live." Without it, they were just breaking even, making just enough to keep the bills from overwhelming them. And that was surviving. *Living* meant going beyond: taking care of needs and then going further.

One year gave them six thousand dollars extra. And the six thousand dollars gave them the ability to do something they wanted to do. In essence, the year produced the ability to do something they wanted to —

worth six thousand dollars.

In a very basic way, what they did with these six thousand dollars accounted for the year.

From when he started working at twenty-five, they saved the six thousand dollars for a down payment on a house. That was what they'd decided to do when they first married, and they stuck to it.

After five years and thirty thousand dollars plus compound interest, they were able to get a mortgage and purchase their modest, one-family house.

After that, they spent the next four years — thirty through thirty-three — fixing it up. They put in a new kitchen, redid the ceiling in the dining room, put down heavy carpeting on the second floor, and built a deck.

The next year — thirty-four — they redid the attic and converted it into a bedroom for their older daughter.

With the house settled, they were able to spend thirty-five on other things. They bought an almost-new car: a six-month-old company car from Buick with two thousand miles on it.

Now they were able to buy extras. Thirty-six was used to buy a new, eight-candle silver *leichter* for his wife. He'd been wanting to get it for the longest time, and now, finally, was the opportunity. They also got — at his *wife's* insistence — a silver menorah and *esrog* box for himself.

With the six thousand dollars from thirty-seven, they were able to do something they'd always wanted to. The family went to Eretz Yisrael for two weeks over Sukkos:

they spent Yom Tov in a hotel, and then had almost a week of touring afterwards. The trip was nothing less than beautiful.

Thirty-eight paid for something they needed: their oldest son's bar mitzvah, with a kiddush and a beautiful affair on the night of the bar mitzvah.

With thirty-nine they were able to replace things that had always been a bother. They bought a new, ready-made sukkah and brand new *schach* and hired a carpenter to build them a *shlak* off the back of their house.

Their old sukkah had been a couple of old boards nailed together, and the *schach* had been branches pruned off trees by the Parks Department.

With forty, they were able to extend a little. They bought a brand new Voyager mini-van, loaded with everything. Power windows and locks, two air bags, front-wheel drive, six cylinders, anti-lock brakes, digital heat and air, and an expensive tape and CD deck.

He had thirty-six months to pay for it in a special deal, so forty-one and forty-two went towards this, too.

In forty-three they bought new furniture. They hadn't bought anything new since their *chasunah*, and it was beginning to show.

They bought a dining-room set: ten chairs and a table, a couch — Castro Convertible — and a couple chairs to go with it. They also picked up semi-used kitchen chairs for four hundred dollars.

Forty-four and forty-five were used to pay for another

need: their daughter's *chasunah.*

Technically, when you think about it, the years of Gedalia are material: the bare walls of the house are his twenty-five to twenty-nine. The kitchen, the ceiling of the dining room, the carpet upstairs, and the deck are his thirty to thirty-three. The redone attic is his thirty-four. And the old car, his thirty-five...

Things don't usually seem this way because our salaries aren't usually divided up so evenly into basic expenditures and non-necessities.

But yet... "This year we made a bar mitzvah, so the car will have to wait for next year." Next year will produce the money that will pay for our new car.

But if that is what we're planning for the year, then looking back, that is how we're going to account for that year. And a year truly cannot be accounted for by its acquisitions.

Acquisitions are material. Time is not.

True Success

*W*HY ME? Yankel Naddowitz could only wonder. Why did it have to be me?

Here he was, fifty-one years old, and a total failure. His financial state was terrible. He was no better off than he had been when he was twenty-five and in *kollel*.

He still could barely pay his rent and feed and clothe his family. And he still had to work long hours just to keep his paper supply business making some sort of profit.

Why couldn't he be like all his friends from yeshiva? he wondered with a touch of bitterness. Somehow *they* all found ways to live comfortable lives. *They* were all able to support their sons and sons-in-law in *kollel*.

And he...

Yankel didn't bother completing the thought.

Even if he was destined to be a failure, he couldn't understand why it had to be on such a wide spectrum.

Socially, he got a D minus. When people made *chasu-nahs*, his was always one of those names that got taken off the list when the *ba'al simchah* realized expenses were running too high. And that was if he was even on the list.

In shul, after twenty years as a faithful member, he didn't get one bit of recognition. Maybe he'd get a *pesichah* once in a while, and a *chamishi* here and there. But a *shelishi*? Forget about it. The only time he got one of those was when he bought it on a Monday or Thursday.

No one could even remember his name.

"Yankel...is it Lefkowitz?"

"But surely, Mr. Rabinowitz..."

"Of course, Mr. Chaimowitz."

People were always apologizing for getting mixed up.

Maybe he really was a nobody...

And his kids...

They would probably end up doing nothing more than joining his own business.

"Naddowitz *and Sons* Paper Supplies," he would call it...

And here he was at fifty-one... What did he have to look forward to? Getting older?

At his age, there was little hope that his business would suddenly prosper. In all probability, things would continue to go just as they had gone until now. His friends would continue driving their Lexuses and dining in Weisses. And he...he'd keep driving his '84 Reliant-K and eating out in Moishe's Pizza and Falafel.

They would continue to make a very *lot* of money in their businesses in Manhattan. And he would continue to make a very *little* money selling his paper goods around Brooklyn.

That was just how it was going to be...

There had been other disappointments in life, certainly. But this was different. This was disappointment in a greater sense. This was total.

He felt as if he had spent all those hard years scraping off one of those instant lottos, and now, finally, he was beginning to make out the words, "Sorry, try again." Only in this game there was no second chance.

But yet...sometimes he'd think differently. Sometimes things didn't seem so bad after all.

He was beginning to understand that the outcome of what you did, the end result of your actions, wasn't something your efforts alone determined; it wasn't something you had the power to control.

You can do everything: you can set up the most brilliant business deal, with plans for exactly how to buy merchandise and then distribute it at great profits... But whether or not it's actually going to happen — whether or not it's actually going to go through — isn't in your hands.

You can manufacture the cutest gimmick, and it can

be parallel to or even better than another one that has just been a sellout. But whether or not people will actually buy yours isn't in your hands to determine.

And it seemed to work the same way with children, too. You can do everything to set your children on the road to accomplishment. But whether or not they are actually *going* to accomplish isn't in your hands. It's not something that your efforts alone can determine.

None of Yankel's friends were significantly smarter than he was. Not one. And none of them had put more effort into their own businesses than he had. Not one.

It was simply that they had been given *siyata dishemaya* to enable their business deals to actually go through and their businesses to prosper.

And you know, he thought, if that was so — if results aren't the direct result of our actions, but rather the result of *siyata dishemaya* — how could end results be considered success? How could this be the way to measure achievement?

And when he thought a bit more, another idea occurred to him: Life *had* to have difficulties in it. If life were a wonderland, with everything going exactly as we wanted, with life being wishful and play-like, without any difficulties and without things going wrong...what would it be like?

Somehow, life without difficulties seemed lacking in a very large way.

Difficulties give purpose. Doing what you are supposed to be doing *despite* the difficulties holding you back, doing what is expected of you *despite* the tough circumstances you are in, makes life purposeful.

And that could be counted as achievement.

Could he say he had accomplished all he'd wanted to in life? No, he couldn't. But when success was measured in a different way, he was most definitely better off than he had thought.

A lot better off.

Our Children

BY MOST STANDARDS, Yisroel Sternberg's life was extremely rough.

When he was all of seven years old, his father died, leaving his mother, himself, and his two sisters with practically nothing.

After three years of barely surviving, his mother married a man with four children. But still, their financial situation didn't really improve.

And then there was the family friction. Yisroel just couldn't get along with his stepfather. He had tried to make things work out, he really had. But it was impossible. Their personalities clashed, and they fought over everything. As a result, he never really felt close to his mother, either.

Finally, five years later — at fifteen — he went to an out-of-town yeshiva.

"Things will be better there," he had reasoned. "After

all, if you're with the same guys all day, you've got to get close to them."

But things didn't work out that way. He wasn't outgoing, and people didn't come over to talk to him.

A year-and-a-half later, at the advice of his rebbe, he switched to another, smaller yeshiva.

But there, although he got to know the guys, he didn't really like them. They weren't his type. His rebbe was nice...but although he never said it, Yisroel could see that he was too busy to listen to his problems.

In six months, he decided it was time to leave, and the next *zeman* he went to a different, local yeshiva.

But he soon realized that this one was similar to his first yeshiva. It was too big and he was getting lost. The *hanhalah* barely even knew he existed.

And there was another thing bothering him. Even the people who did know him — his mother, his stepfather, and his few friends — were negative towards him. They always criticized him. They were always telling him what to do and when and how to do it. Why couldn't they just give him a few inches to breathe?

He didn't have anywhere to turn...

At twenty, Yisroel left yeshiva and started working. He got a job driving a truck for a wine wholesaler and settled into it.

After a year, he was introduced to a girl in a similar situation, and not too long afterwards they were married.

His marriage never really hit it off. At times they'd get into senseless arguments that went on and on. But because he was working such long hours driving the truck, and his wife worked equally hard behind the counter in a shoe store, they rarely had the strength to argue. Usually they'd just have supper, talk a little, go to sleep, and wake up in the morning again.

But there was one thing he was thankful for. And that was that, close to two years after their marriage, his wife had given birth to adorable little Yeruchom. There were no words to describe the joy he had, and how much his little son meant to him.

Whenever he had a chance, he would just sit and watch little Yeruchom. He'd watch as the baby struggled to turn over, and then when he struggled to get up on his hands and knees...

As Yisrocl watched little Yeruchom growing up, there was one thing he promised himself. True, he'd had a rough life, and there was little hope that he would ever do anything worthwhile with it. But for his son...for his son, things were going to be different. If there was one thing Yisroel would do with his life, it would be to give his son the things he hadn't had when he was growing up.

For himself, driving a truck ten hours a day was fine. But his son... No — his son wouldn't have to struggle to make it without help and encouragement. He would give

Yeruchom all the attention and care that he knew was needed...

This is where "Yisroel Sternberg" is today. A story like his occurs only from time to time. But yet the *feelings* he has, although perhaps to a lesser degree are, in fact, quite prevalent.

It is common for us to disregard our own need for accomplishment in life and put our main efforts into helping our children gain a high level of achievement.

Can we love our children more than we love ourselves? Certainly. Can we give them more than we give ourselves? Absolutely.

But we shouldn't make them the *only* source of meaning and purpose in our lives. Because, in fact...they aren't.

Self-confidence

*Y*ONAH WONDERED WHAT THE *MASHGIACH* could have in mind as he pushed open the swinging doors in back of the *beis medrash* and made his way towards the office.

The new *zeman* had just started and he had been trying to get "into" *Shenayim Ochazin.*

At age twenty-two and fifth-year *beis medrash*, he had finally made it to being a bit of an *eltere bachur* in the yeshiva. Him, an *eltere bachur*? But that's the way things were...

He had come to the yeshiva in ninth grade, and now after eight full years he had finally reached the top of the ladder.

Softly he knocked on the *mashgiach*'s door.

"Have a seat, Yonah," Rabbi Silverman suggested as Yonah stepped inside.

He finished making notations in a roll book spread

out on his desk, then looked up. "Yonah, I need your assistance. There's a new *bachur* coming tonight that I'd like you to befriend. He is a fine and bright boy. But the problem is that he's a bit stuck in his shell. If you can somehow help him open up and be accepted by his *shiur*, you will be doing him a very great favor.

"He had a hard time in the yeshiva he was in," Rabbi Silverman explained. "He wasn't accepted, and as time went on he grew more and more apart from his class-mates. If you can change this trend and get him back up on his feet, you can have a positive impact on the rest of his life."

"What should I do first?" Yonah asked.

"The way to begin, I've found, is to have a *seder* with him," Rabbi Silverman said. "That way you're able to build the relationship up slowly, and you don't have to create opportunities. His name is Boruch — Boruch Seransky. Is there anything else you'd like to know?"

"I guess not," Yonah replied. "I'll give it a try..."

"Good," Rabbi Silverman said, putting his hand down softly on Yonah's. "Let me know how it goes."

It was right before night *seder* when Yonah remem-bered about his meeting with Rabbi Silverman that af-ternoon.

He glanced around the *beis medrash*.

That...that had to be him, he observed, noting a new *bachur*, fifteen or sixteen years old, in the back of the room, occasionally glancing around uncomfortably from behind a pair of thick glasses.

Yonah went up to him.

"Shalom aleichem," he said. "My name is Yonah Menkin. Are you Boruch Seransky?"

"Yes," Boruch nodded.

"Do you have *chavrusos* yet?"

"No," Boruch replied with a shrug.

Here was the opportunity.

"Oh. So why don't we have a *seder* at night, say, from after supper until night *seder*? Is that okay with you?"

"Okay," Boruch responded, his eyes moving from Yonah to the floor and back again.

"Do you have everything straightened out, you know, your room and everything else?"

Boruch nodded.

The conversation wasn't going anywhere.

"Very nice," Yonah said. "I'll tell you the truth. I'm in middle of something and I have to make this short. But if you need anything, feel free to come over and ask, okay?"

Boruch nodded again.

"See you tomorrow night."

Yonah returned to the middle of the *beis medrash*.

Rabbi Silverman wasn't exaggerating when he said that he's in his shell, he sighed. What was it that made Boruch feel so uneasy when he spoke to him? He couldn't understand.

Later that evening, Yonah reflected on his meeting with Boruch.

Self-confidence is an interesting thing, he mused. Anyone can have it. And its benefits are great. Socially, it makes all the difference. In work — any type of work — it takes self-confidence to achieve success.

Yet so many people lack it. And usually for no other reason than feelings of inferiority built up in childhood.

It seemed so ridiculous.

True, he knew, self-confidence is good only up to a point. Being icily confident isn't necessarily a *ma'aleh*. There are times when you *should* feel uneasy. But somehow, he thought, it is better to have too much self-confidence than to have too little...

The next evening Boruch was waiting for Yonah when he came inside the *beis medrash*.

"How are you?" Yonah asked as he made his way to his seat.

"Fine," Boruch responded, checking uneasily to make sure his *payos* were behind his ears.

Yonah sat down and put his gemara on a *shtender*. "Is there anything specific you want to learn?" he asked.

"No," Boruch replied.

"How about *Kitzur Shulchan Aruch*? It should be *geshmak*."

Boruch nodded.

As they began to learn, Yonah noticed that Boruch would shrug his shoulders and turn to him whenever he couldn't figure something out.

Different, he noted, from the guy he'd learned with last *zeman*. That *bachur* had always said, "I'm going to have *peshat* before *seder* is over tonight. Just you wait."

And his former *chavrusah* usually *did* end up having a *peshat*, while Boruch didn't.

Their *seder* was almost over, and Yonah decided to make an attempt at conversation.

"*Nu*, so how was your first day in yeshiva? How was the *shiur*?" he asked.

"It was good," Boruch replied uneasily.

"Was the *shiur* similar to what you're used to?"

"Yes," Boruch nodded.

After a week, Yonah went back to Rabbi Silverman.

"Rebbe," he said, "I'm not making progress. Things aren't moving."

"It's still early," Rabbi Silverman assured him. "Keep doing what you're doing, and come back to me in a month."

Yonah nodded, but he wasn't so sure.

Another few weeks slowly went by, and still, Yonah had nothing to show for them. It was becoming frustrating. He had tried everything: being funny, being serious, being encouraging, being demanding, and he still couldn't get a solid response out of Boruch. Boruch would just shrug his shoulders and give a meek half-smile.

Maybe the reason it's difficult to gain self-confidence, it occurred to Yonah one night after their *seder* had ended, is because insecurity works in a cycle. People who lack confidence don't speak up thinking: "I won't speak up. I'm just not one of those guys who do."

But truthfully, it is only because they never did speak up, that they never do.

They never have, because they never do. And they never do, because they never have.

If people could only muster up the courage to break this cycle just once, understanding that it's worth looking foolish one time to take away their fear of doing so...

He sighed.

And besides, he wondered, how would other people know if someone has confidence or not? Nobody can automatically tell. When Boruch came to the yeshiva, he could have been the most confident guy around, and no one would have known any different. So why can't people like Boruch just make-believe that they're confident?

It was becoming obvious that the words of confidence he was giving Boruch weren't penetrating deeply enough. They seemed to be bouncing off his deep-rooted feelings of inferiority.

Well, there is one more approach I can use, he decided at last.

During lunch the next day, Yonah made his move.

He went over to Boruch, who was sitting a bit further down the table than the rest of the *shiur*.

"Boruch," he said, "how about if we take a walk after lunch? Is it okay with you? I want to discuss something."

Boruch nodded.

"I'll wait upstairs."

Five minutes later Boruch came upstairs, and they started walking. For the first few minutes, Yonah didn't say anything.

"Boruch," he finally began. "I want to tell you a story, which incidentally happened in our very own yeshiva about eight years ago. At that time, there was a *bachur* in the ninth grade named Tzvi, who was a very with-it guy. But yet, he was someone who didn't have any confidence at all. And he was even a bit withdrawn. Rabbi Bender, who was then the ninth-grade rebbe, noticed this and one day after *seder*, he called him over...

"Tzvi," Rabbi Bender said, "I want to discuss something with you."

Tzvi nodded.

"I want to discuss the importance of being confident — the importance of knowing that you're important.

"Tzvi, many years ago I had a good friend named Yisroel, or Sruli. Anyway, he had been with us in kollel for quite some time, and because of circumstances, he had to go out and get a job.

"He found a promising job opening and arranged an interview. But he had never had an interview before, and he was terribly nervous.

" 'What do you think I'm going to be asked?' he was constantly saying to his friends. 'What do you think the interviewer is going to ask?'

"He went around memorizing little flash cards and making up mock interviews. I'll tell you, the more he asked, the more nervous he got.

"Anyway, he came over to me on the morning of the big day and asked me what he should wear. He was the most nervous person I had seen in a very, very long time.

" 'Sruli,' I told him, 'You're sitting here getting nervous thinking about how to act in an interview, and the interviewer himself is sitting in his own house worrying about what he's going to ask you! He's a new interviewer and very unsure about whether he'll be able to do it right. So both of you are worrying about each other!'

"I could see he wasn't very convinced that this was actually how it was.

" 'Okay,' I told him. 'Let's even say that your interviewer will be confident during your interview this afternoon, and when he asks you the questions he won't be nervous. Is that a reason for you to now lose your confidence?

" 'If I could guarantee that your interviewer would be just as nervous as you are, you wouldn't be nervous, agreed?'

"Sruli nodded.

" 'So if he keeps his composure, why should you lose the confidence you already have?

" 'And besides,' I told him, 'it's a lot easier to talk to an interviewer who's calm, sitting easily in a chair. That way he'll hear you out — he'll give you a chance to really explain yourself. And that way you can ask him all about the job he wants you to take.'

"In the end, Sruli went to the interview and got the job.

"Tzvi," Rabbi Bender said, "I understand that you don't feel comfortable speaking up in shiur. I really do. And I understand that you don't feel comfortable speaking up amongst your friends. But Tzvi, you have to. Tzvi, you must. You can't afford to live your whole life scared about what people might think of you. You won't get anywhere. Not in learning and not in any other field..."

"And," Yonah said, "Tzvi did speak up. He took the conversation to heart and made changes. It wasn't easy for him. But little by little he forced himself to do things he had felt uneasy doing before. The more he did it, the less uneasy he felt doing it. And the more he did it, the more he felt that he *should* be doing it, because doing so made him feel better about himself.

"And now, if I may say so myself, a full eight years later, Tzvi is taking care of himself."

Yonah stopped a second.

"I never did tell you that my name is Yonah *Tzvi*, did I," he said.

They slowly made their way back to the yeshiva.

Yonah wasn't sure if he had helped Boruch or not. But as time went on, he could slowly see Boruch making himself heard more often.

It seemed that Rabbi Silverman also noticed the changes, and one day after *minchah* he called Yonah over.

"Yonah, you're doing a great job!" he said. "I can really see a difference on Boruch's face! Keep it up."

But to Yonah, it didn't seem as if he deserved a compliment. He was only doing what he had to do. It was nothing less than an obligation of his, to pass along to someone else the advice Rabbi Bender had given him.

That Bit of Thought

*I*RVING GARR(FINKEL) DOESN'T GO OUT MUCH. At eighty-six, living alone in his twelfth-story apartment in Starret City, a trip down is something he just doesn't feel all that comfortable doing.

He would much rather lie on his bed with his feet propped up on a few feather pillows, listening to "fifties" music.

Besides, why should he go out at all? He gets the daily paper and his groceries delivered to his door, and he has his good friend, Max Ruby(nstein), in the apartment across the hall for company. And, as for his health, he has a local doctor stop by every few weeks to give him a routine checkup.

He spends a good part of his day keeping house and preparing his meals and medications. Sometimes he even rearranges the light furniture in his living room — the square table he picked up about thirty-five years ago at an auction somewhere in the Midwest, the plant his daughter sent him for his eightieth birthday, and that big, old easy chair that came with the first house they'd bought — to give the apartment a different look.

But most of all, it's that big transistor radio that keeps him busy — the needle right on WSLW and the "golden oldies."

Recently, though, he has started spending some of his time just thinking. No, not really thinking — that wasn't the right word. It is more, kind of, wondering.

You know, wondering what it's all about.

He's lived a full life. He's seen a dozen presidents come and he's seen a dozen presidents go. He's seen years of war and he's seen years of peace. He's seen years of prosperity and he's seen years of deprivation. What was all this for?

It is beginning to seem as if life is actually part of some greater plan, that life is something like the spin of a big wheel. You start at the bottom, make your way to the top, and then slowly wind your way back down to the bottom again. But what is the turn for? What's it all about? He's been wondering...

Lately, when he looks out his window, he sees the things outside in a somewhat different perspective. It is beginning to seem as if the world is a place that he was put *into* — a place that was pre-made exclusively to meet his and all humanity's requirements.

He had never thought much about the maple tree down near the curb below. But now it's started to seem so much more purposeful. He always knew that trees use carbon dioxide and produce oxygen. Nothing ever seemed unusual about that. Now trees are beginning to look like big oxygen tanks powered by something people don't need — carbon dioxide.

And it seems that another purpose of trees is to be like big venetian blinds. It starts getting hotter in the spring, and out their leaves come. It starts getting colder in the fall, and off they go. It seems trees try to do their job better by spreading out and covering as much space as they can...

The fir is different. It keeps its leaves all year around — and it doesn't spread out. Firs grow their branches thick and very close together, as opposed to leaving room between them. While most trees are wider at the top than at the bottom, firs are wider at the bottom than at the top.

Maybe all the differences have a common denominator: the different needs they serve. Maybe the purpose of the fir *isn't* to shade people as other trees do. Maybe their purpose is to give life and color to the seemingly lifeless winter. That would explain why firs keep their green leaves all year around. And it would explain why their branches don't spread out, and why they grow their branches thick and all the way to the ground. And perhaps it even explains why they have prickly leaves: to keep people at an observational distance. Maybe that's why they grow in a conical structure: so when snow falls on their branches, it won't weigh enough to break them.

That article he'd read a long time ago about why trees in forests grow their branches higher off the ground than do trees in cities also makes sense. The article had explained that it was because trees extend their branches toward available sunlight. In cities, sunlight is available everywhere. But in forests, it is only available very high off the ground.

Interestingly, other convenient things happen because of this. First, the branches of both trees in cities and trees in forests end up growing at heights convenient for people. In cities, where people need room only to walk, branches start growing a few feet over the average person's head. But in forests, where people often travel by horse, the branches start a lot higher up. And second, it takes a lot more forest trees to shade a specific area than city trees. Maybe that is because in a city, an excess of tree trunks would impede people's movements. But in a forest the extra tree trunks provide shelter for animals. Maybe that is why the need for sunlight affects the growth of the trees.

The water that fills a well, too, is beginning to take on a different dimension. He always knew that there are underground streams. But now they seem much more a part of a master plan. They provide people with water in places without above-ground streams. And maybe the water is *under*ground because otherwise it would get in people's way; during a heavy downpour the streams would converge and cause damage. This also explains why the earth freezes only to a certain depth: to keep the underwater streams from freezing. In addition, these days, with modern plumbing, streams are unnecessary in most places. They seem to be saying, "If you need me, I'm here. If not, I'm out of your way."

Maybe...

And come to think of it, fruits and vegetables also seem to be set aside specifically for people to eat. Isn't that why they change their colors when they become ripe — to show us when we can eat them?

Natural deposits like coal and oil also seem to be, quite literally, deposits. Things that were deposited — to be *withdrawn* by people. There aren't any deposits of useless blue gels throughout the world, he's noted...

Older people think. They think about themselves, the world, and life in general.

They have seen it all: the Roaring Twenties, the Depression thirties, and the war-time forties. They've seen the cold-war fifties, the rebellious sixties, and the "liberated" seventies. They've watched the prosperous eighties, and now the slow-starting nineties.

They've seen good times and they've seen bad times, happy times and sad times. They've seen generations grow up and generations pass away. And naturally, they begin to think and wonder. What is it all about? What is the purpose of it all?

And when they come to a conclusion, they have to assess how much of their past coincides with this purpose, and how much doesn't.

Being older may induce this kind of thought.

But do we really have to be older to think about it?

An Afterthought...

ON A WARM EVENING IN LATE MAY 1990, a yeshiva *bachur* began writing a few of his thoughts and reflections into essays. Looking back, he doesn't know what he'd hoped to get out of it, but just the same, he'd begun.

Now, following the laws of practicality, the writings should have taken this route: in a bottom drawer for a couple of weeks, then into the back of an old file cabinet, neatly packed in a pocketless folder and labeled in pen: "Writings — May 1990."

There wasn't any real future in it. The points dealt with were basic, and the way they were conveyed was quite blunt. It was something that would be of interest later in life, but not something that would appeal to other people.

But he was encouraged.

"Any new essays?"

"What are you working on now?"

He continued writing. He edited. Rewrote. Edited. Rewrote. Time passed, years passed, and after five long years, there was enough material to be published as a book.

That yeshiva *bachur* is this very author. Without the encouragement I received, this book wouldn't have been written. And with a fair dose of *dis*couragement, the whole idea of writing would have quickly come to an end.

"Maybe it's not for me, after all. It takes years to develop writing skills," I'd have reasoned.

I would have put down my pen, put away my spiral notebook (reflecting, years later, "I once tried writing, myself, but it just didn't go") and that would have been it. The potential of this book would have never been reached.

Truthfully, though, it was only because I continued to write that I was able to build on my existing thoughts and arrive at points that are possibly worth writing about.

And you know, sometimes I kind of wonder... If I had stopped writing because I hadn't received encouragement, would it have been the right thing to do? Would it have been the correct course to follow?

Writing has been a learning experience. With effort and determination, we can bring about results. But only if we are willing to look away from a lack of *en*couragement and an excess of *dis*couragement, and give it a serious, motivated try.